T0082823

narrow
escapes

Narrow
Escapes

A Poetic Diary of the Coronavirus Pandemic

Tanure Ojaide

Spears Books

SPEARS BOOKS
AN IMPRINT OF SPEARS MEDIA PRESS LLC
7830 W. Alameda Ave, Suite 103-247
Denver, CO 80226
United States of America

First Published in the United States of America in 2021 by Spears Books
www.spearsmedia.com
info@spearsmedia.com
@spearsbooks

Information on this title: www.spearsmedia.com/narrow-escapes
© 2021 Tanure Ojaide
All rights reserved.

No part of this publication may be reproduced, distributed, or transmitted in any form or by any means, including photocopying, recording, or other electronic or mechanical methods, without the prior written permission of the publisher, except in the case of brief quotations embodied in critical reviews and certain other noncommercial uses permitted by copyright law. For permission requests, write to the publisher, addressed "Attention: Permissions Coordinator," at the address above.

Library of Congress Control Number: 2021932624

ISBN: 9781942876779 (Paperback)
ISBN: 9781942876786 (eBook)
Also available in Kindle format

Cover art: Emedjo Orhue (Hunter Masquerade), Plastograph 22 x 17 cm by Bruce Onobrakpeya
Cover designed by Doh Kambem
Designed and typeset by Spears Media Press LLC

Distributed globally by African Books Collective (ABC)
www.africanbookscollective.com

For my daughter, Amreghe Ojaide Poku

Contents

PREFACE

I started these poems focused on the experience of the novel coronavirus, otherwise known as the Covid-19, after I had just completed a volume of poems titled *To Those Who Love Me*. I was reflecting on what next to do when the coronavirus started to flare up in the United States. At the time that one heard about it in Wuhan in China, the United States had not started to take the pandemic seriously. I had travelled to Nigeria from the United States on February 27, 2020, through New York and Paris. With JFK, New York, and CDG, Paris, not having any form of screening, I was surprised upon landing in Abuja, Nigeria, to see airport workers wearing face covers, now popularly called masks. At Abuja, as we came down the plane before the Customs line, every arriving passenger's temperature had to be taken and each person had to fill a long form about contacts, phone numbers, and where one would stay. The day before our arrival, the first case of the novel coronavirus had been detected in Nigeria—an Italian who had gone in through Turkish Airlines to Lagos. The government had before the first case put in place contact tracing of those who would test positive for the novel coronavirus. By the time I was travelling back to Charlotte on March 8, Paris and New York still remained unconcerned about the coronavirus which had been declared a pandemic at that time. By March 10, the American Government started to take things seriously after a rather unserious attitude before then. Faculty, staff, and students in universities began to be jittery. By the end of that week, universities started to close and we were asked to move our teaching online. That is the background to this collection of poems.

The poems are thus my response to the Covid-19 pandemic. The collection is a spiritual journey to better understand the meaning of life. Poetry is a spiritual journey for many poets and readers and through it one could have a better understanding of life. It is not the pursuit of material success alone that ultimately matters since one cannot carry wealth or success to the afterlife but enshrining in humanity the virtues of compassion, love, generosity, sensitivity, and sacrifice in our lives. These virtues will make one to be remembered for good. One realizes that life is transient and helping others rather than only the self brings a lot of fulfillment. The Covid-19 pandemic is in some ways a leveler of people irrespective of class, race, or ideology and makes everyone realize his or her humanity. In a time such as the pandemic's, for me, writing poetry affords me the time to deeply reflect on the vagaries of human experiences across geographical space and different cultures. It distracts me from not only psychological but also other types of stress. One can say, it is therapy to me. I hope those who read poems on the pandemic will also see them as such in addition to their aesthetic value.

I chose to have the diary form so that the poems will be diary entries that are relatively short. I tried to communicate and at the same time be as poetic as I can. Each poem contributes to the overall collection which I have conceived as a quilt or a nest to which I gathered different materials to build. Each day's feeling adds something new and perhaps different to make up the overall pandemic experience. I have left the poems in the order in which they were written; hence the dates progressing from early March onwards. Thus, there is an emotional progression in the poems which reflect the trajectory of the pandemic itself in emotional terms: from the time one heard of the novel coronavirus devastating faraway Wuhan, China, to its ravaging of Europe, especially Italy, Spain, and the United Kingdom, through New York State to the gradual infection of other States in the United States and other countries such as Brazil, Ecuador, India, South Africa, and Russia. April and the first half of May were very grim. The early successes in combating the virus led to the false confidence that the worst was over and the cry for the lifting of lockdown which many American States did in a precipitate fashion. And many folks in those states behaved as if the virus had been defeated. The second wave started. Of interest is the argument between those who want to take care of their livelihood and those who want to take care of their lives. No doubt, the poems reflect my personal response to the entire period and they mimic in a way the daily and weekly graphs of the scourge of Covid-19.

Throughout the period, I was inspired by my muse, Aridon, the god of memory and poetic inspiration in my Urhobo culture. These poetic entries in the diary are gifts to me. I did not know the next poem I would write until it came. Usually, I went to bed and got awakened sometime with a nudge to write down what constitutes the poems. I had to wake and write—often not sleeping well to take advantage of the inspirational spell. Aridon will not leave me alone and I have to obey the call.

During the entire period of the writing, I sent each day's entry or entries to Enajite Ojaruega who read them and sent me comments, informed by her intuitive understanding of poetry, to strengthen them, if possible. Her delight in the poems made me feel that I was doing a worthwhile work. She teased me that I was using writing as therapy, which I didn't mind as long as Aridon kept me active. I am grateful for her support. I also want to acknowledge Mathias Orhero and Saeedat Aliyu who also read and commented on the entire collection.

I hope those who read the collection will not only relive the period but also share in the experiences expressed. I also hope the beauty I have attempted to create out of the terrible experience makes meaning and makes us more human to embrace the virtues that will make our lives impact positively on others. I hope they gain fulfillment in these virtues and also enjoy the "entries" as sheer poetic delight.

Tanure Ojaide
Charlotte, NC, USA
November, 2020

1

The World Revolves Around a Virus

The world revolves around a novel virus.
Time the minutest of things caught attention.
Worse still, it hedges all into quarantine.
This is terrible, tiny to invisibility
yet poaching the known world into panic-
stricken enclaves for self-preservation.
For a change the smallest of things
unleashes a stampede. Terrible, really so!
Fear tiny things and their mortal rage!

2

Every Year Cannot be Normal

In a normal year, we celebrate
birthdays and burials, take titles,
and gather to party and dance.
We live a charmed life; demigods
who know tomorrow and more.
This year hasn't remained normal.

Every year cannot always be normal.
There are times for tantrums between
lovers. Now it has never been as bad.
We who love change and variety
now have more than we can handle—
something strange as never before!

In a normal year leaps out
this abnormality. An invisible
virus terrorizes the world, routs
the powerful from their comfort;
the weak further humiliated
by the plethora of failings.

So many postponements
and cancellations to put
on hold life as we knew it.
Who knows tomorrow?
Here we are in a new day
failing tests of preparedness.
Demigods fail their forecasts.

3

Flood of Fire

You wake to grimmer news.
The blaze spreads beyond the imagination—
nowhere to escape to
that's not already drowned
in the terrible flood of fire.

4

Not the Common Chinese Brand

(March 19, 2020)

We got so used to Chinese brands
and saw this as nothing that will last.
If shoes, you wouldn't walk a meter;
if a vehicle, it wouldn't move a mile.
And so many dismissed the brand fake;
a hoax until the entire world got smitten!

It was a perfect setup: a blaze
without borders fueled from all sides;
fire leaped as it had never before
consuming green and brown leaves
as never happened before. War of
another kind, terrible by all accounts;
mortality made it serious business.

From now on every nation cares for itself.
This is no Chinese brand to break down
before leaving its borders; it has acquired
German engineering, Italian fickleness, and
Ayatollah's deep-rooted stubbornness!
The global blaze consumes all in its path.

5

The Riddle of Tomorrow

(March 20, 2020)

Day dawns and the dirge intensifies.
The riddle of tomorrow remains unsolved;
hence death continues to poach a number.

The old swear by what they have never seen;
the youths defy fate but can't find adventures.
Patient 17 succumbs to the ogre's skirmish.

Only yesterday a doctor couldn't pull himself
from the echoes that stilled his breath;
no one plays safe pranks with Corona!

Tears to bed, tears at dawn for numbers—
the trail lengthens in a magical route
the fetish minutest of beings litters.

The statistics stagger along calamitous routes;
the virus slithers beyond the visible path.
Who now understands the riddle of tomorrow?

Day dawns and the sun proffers dim light,
the face in a grey hood all day;
cold neither here nor there but filling everywhere.

When young and old, men and women stay indoors,
abandon the roads and open spaces to the littlest,
the world surely pays reparations for disrespect.

6

Who Prays for Rain

Who prayed for rain
drowned in the gift deluge.

Those who seek individual privacy
now have got their sovereign spaces.

It has taken a spirit imp no effort
to force through the self-isolation.

7

A Show of Power

The American Airforce took to the air
but its insulted target eluded radar detection—
it's not every foe that gives itself out;
everyone, however small, exercises survival instincts.

The small one taunts the most powerful;
it draws the hulk to an open combat—
one whose wings fly faster than a flash
and the invisible one sticks to the surface.

The stealth jet fighters scramble into the air,
presidential orders behind an incredible force
but they fly blindfolded into great heights with
out encounter. It takes more than might to prevail.

Scraaam! Rather than crash a capitalist toy,
the Commander-in-Chief recalls the flying demigods
and on the nose of the B52 and flyers a stain;
the metamorphosed littlest taunting a superpower!

Manhood has nothing to do with mere size
and for all the braggadocio of inexhaustible resources,
the loaded Airforce falls flat. The small one
thrives on the impotence of the hulk.

8

Mother Earth Sheds Her Crushing Load

(March 21, 2020)

The earth can no longer grow to expand
beyond her size and acquire more capacity
to bear all the children and their needs.
Something has to give way on either end—
the provider has to turn into a superhuman
or benefactors have to decrease in number.
Humans are populating every crack and hole
as if helpless for every open space to breed.
With nowhere else to discover or uncover,
no corner free for storage or occupation,
both earth and folks have come to a bind.
And so every new birth breaks the back
with a mouth gorging more than is there.
If billions are ravaging everywhere
on her back, poaching sore her bosom,
what else than seek relief by any means?
See the tantrums that disquiet everyone!
Let earth shake off the backbreaking load
to live without pain and breathe free!

9

Obanikoro Chooses to Appear

When things are so normal—
scheduled events, weddings, birthdays;
what folks choose to love and celebrate
to sweeten things they have to swallow
and refresh for faster results than wait
too long in a life too unclear to bank on—
Obanikoro* chooses to appear to seek
attention and respect by upturning things.

This is its own choosing, coming
when flights have to cancel a week
to the transnational tryst of a decade;
coming before those cooped in cold
have the chance to sun themselves
after the weather changed with time.
Obanikoro downs planes, closes borders,
empties workplaces and streets indoors.

Obanikoro appears when not wanted
but chooses to make an idle point
of self-regulating manners as normal.
It takes one to disrupt the indulgence
of many; it only takes the unexpected
to turn upside down the plans of those
who see themselves as demigods.
Off guard and so assured of tomorrow,
Obanikoro comes to test overconfidence.

* Obanikoro: flippant Nigerian/Yoruba name for the novel coronavirus.

10

Koro

(March 22, 2020)

Koro* summons all nations for a contest,
its own kind of Olympics, rather Para-Olympics—
the able-bodied flying from the North
and those challenged limping from the South.
What a sight, the global assembly of talents
brandishing enough flags to clothe the naked!

It turned out every nation that thought
it was so spritely suffers some disability—
the richest and loudest of them all, lame;
the most powerful, a brass trumpet, impotent.
Spectators laughed and taunted them.
The most private of havens penetrated,
infested into wards spilling into streets.

Every contest is a kind of test for all
in the weeks and months to complete.
Those who listen and are so respectful
by nature got it right; it was a sacrifice—
they gathered mystical hands and healed.
Those who had seen themselves better
than the rest of the world retarded;
their failures and mortality astonished.

The public test brought resentment of lords
who had swaggered as if they knew all
but came out lacking so much others have.
It was a surprise the poor and weak of the South
often ridden over by brash ones of the North
scored even better to redefine themselves.
It was not the loud mouths but the medals
that rank winners and losers of the contest.

*Koro: shortened form for Obanikoro, the Nigerian/Yoruba nickname for the novel
coronavirus.

11

World War

(March 23, 2020)

For the first time
in the history of the universe
a real world war.
Not like when a small but big-headed
continent's eggheads—Hitler, Mussolini,
Stalin, Chamberlain, and cousin, Roosevelt—
called their tussle for dominion
WW I and WW II.
That wasn't WW by any measure
but a family feud; internecine.
Now the entire world fights
an invisible enemy;
a real war.
For the first time
a war against an enemy
that no nuclear strikes can eliminate.
Sorry, it has no ideology or race
to rally Allies or liars
for excuse to use the A-bomb;
hence it's no war as known before
but a real WW.

12

Déjà vu

I have always walked through
a ghost town; no human sound
and even birds taking a nap
this early that I am up and alone.

And so it's nothing new
the quarantine of the already
entombed; indoors a lifestyle
now legitimized by necessity.

I never expect children
running out pursued by parents;
I never expect ghosts outdoors;
hence a ghost town is evacuated

and never bustles with faces
the hive in the tomb.
I never expect a swarm outdoors
as if the sun would scorch them.

All the forces have come together
and nothing is strange anymore;
yes, the streets are so empty.
It's the déjà vu! There's no change—

snakes will never move in a group.
There's so much silence;
a sprawling ghost town stares me
in the face on my daily walks.

13

Tomorrow is a Riddle

Tomorrow is a riddle today can't solve.
Bring together all the knowledge of the world
but still tomorrow will defy forecasts of its outcome.

Let them go to Adelphi for the answer,
let them dig to any depth, climb to any height;
the knot eludes the skill of proclaimed craftsmen.

Patients lay on the floor, not hospital beds, in Madrid.
Who steered the Armada wrecked in a home reality—
see exposed the future of an empire in rubble!

Who knew the world would come to witness this,
those with attitude stripped of their swagger?
Who foresaw this contagion of liberal democracy?

Among the despising, I pity who claims premiership.
I do not despise anyone sharing the same planet.
Tomorrow will frog-jump every human to a bizarre rhythm.

14

Infestations Galore

(March 24, 2020)

The charlatans never had it so good,
their doorsteps a traffic of lies
retouched into model manikins for export.

Fake news is so inflammable it consumes
so many that peddle it for fun or malice;
so directionless the world wobbles.

The tabloids easily retool their presses,
print and circulate hogwash as elixir
which by advantage of covers circulates.

Facebook, master communicator, posts
disquieting info—the blaze couldn't
have taken more wings to smother all.

They trend the revival of apothecaries
as street vendors take over storefronts;
everyone a hypochondriac seeking remedies—

chloroquine overdose in Nigeria; hospitals
take over beds virus victims need to survive
and the cure becomes a more lethal disease.

O age of migrants and instant news,
you may have dealt a blow to ignorance
but your gossip flares panic attacks.

There are too many liars as prophets,
a legion of counseling tell-tale archangels
and what fuels here pours from all corners.

Even truth has alternatives; double talk.
How did we come to this pandemic?
Infestations already corroded before corona!

15

Deadly Neighbors

Malaria settled in our midst from the beginning
making death a permanent mischievous neighbor.

Cholera poaches every quarter
and often downs a dirty number.

AIDS still ravages us with love
and every face shadows a ghost.

All sorts of fevers thrive in our midst—
dengue and Lassa lead the charge

intoning the dirge and leading
quite a traffic to the cemetery.

Death dealers have long been neighbors;
we fight them as they stubbornly fight back.

And as if we have not had enough of death
from herdsmen, not enough from afflictions

*kolona varius** arrives to sack a land
already devastated by fearful ones.

*kolona varius: one of the mispronunciations of "coronavirus" in Nigeria.

16

Neither Ancestors nor Citizens

(March 25, 2020)

Another day dawns
and I wait for breaking news.
My heart beats arrhythmically.
Today's reality will be another shock.
The statistics zigzag to another peak—
at this rate it will tip over Mount Everest!
After Manu Dibango, who's next in the toll?
For sure the riddle defies an answer—
there are things we just can't know ahead
and prepare for; if we foreknew everything,
we would wage war against the gods of our fates
wresting from them their omnipotence to show off.

We can forecast the weather. It is early spring
and it barely rains. The sun's no shield anymore.
We can prop up the dollar from dropping.
We see clearly but can't yet untie the knot.
Names spill over extended obituary pages.
In some places they still count the dead;
in other regions counting has lost meaning
because the living are already dead to life
and those dead for lack of proper rites are
wailing in a dire procession through dark alleys
to where they are neither ancestors nor citizens
and so unwelcome. My heart beats irregularly.

17

The End of the World

We have come to the very end of the world
we knew and lived from the beginning of time.
We speak so much of bad dreams in wakeful hours
but here's the nightmare we never experienced.
We complain of siege of our quarters and towns in war
and now an invisible force besieges the entire world.

Everything past was child's play. This is the real
World War. Nobody lives through this and remains
the same taking for granted freedom to embrace,
kiss, make love, and indulge in carefree moments.
Nobody fails to appreciate past habits of lovers
that made this malady an existential tonic;
nobody goes through this panic assault of all times
and fails to shake from its inescapable memory.

Jehovah's Witnesses foresaw this Armageddon
in their creed but not this close but at a later day;
the oracles read it from their seven cowries
but the prescribed sacrifice too steep to offer;
forecasters saw the global dance at a precipice
but none to restrain enough to avert this fall.
Until it engulfed all, no scrambling to foil the blaze
when looking back doesn't take us safely forward.

There's none to blame for the end of the world we knew.
The small ones have arrived to rattle loud mouths;
they have come to test how prepared the faith adopted
to live day by day and not when ambushed from nowhere.
Those obsessed with time failed to see timeless virtues,
those so stuck with restless movement have to shelter in;
those who wouldn't touch others condemned to a distance.

What a nightmare it is, the end of the world we had known!

18

The Business of Life

The heart warms up to the only regularity
of the irregular season—

"Good morning!" comes from home and outside;
we are alone but not lonely.

"Stay safe!" We take care of ourselves
but want those on our minds to be safe too.

Someone makes you laugh so hilariously
you don't pay attention to the last tally.

You pray to the god of fortunate ones to make you
and another live to remember the dark days behind.

And that's life:
in the face of death the business of life.

19

It Cares Not

(March 26, 2020)

Over there in the Niger Delta where I grew up,
they call it the affliction of the affluent who fly,
which bus riders see as where they contract it.
But when the harmattan blaze rages in the forest,
it consumes green and brown leaves on its path.
Folks of different quarters went down with it
as youths who bragged as indomitable lions.

Here where I find myself an immigrant, the rich
call it the affliction of ghettoes, and so pumped up
in their charmed lives they deny its ugly presence
until they stepped into it in the tic-tac-toe after
dancing around the unobstructed global demon.
Now rich and poor, men and women as youths
are part of the statistics peaking beyond Everest.

Call it mean spirited, it cares not. Keep distant
from the mad one pursuing you with a machete!
That's how those who don't believe they can be tagged
for sacrifice or flagellation came to stutter in disbelief.
One day brings forth what has never been seen before;
hence the sage asks the experts: Who knows tomorrow?
The toll of casualties defies counting by experts.

20

Filling the New Ark

There are stampedes into stores and supermarkets
as far apart as Jo'burg, Lagos, and Charlotte
to overfill buggies with essential commodities
to fill the ark to survive the doomed season.
There's been no toilet paper as I move from store
to store; all canned and frozen foods vanished.
One-kilometer-long line snakes to the cashier's desk.
At home millennium compliant refrigerators filled.

Everybody stockpiling more than for now—
pet food, fancy dresses for proscribed carnivals;
so much money to spend than leave for inheritance.
More than enough to sustain one whatever time
it takes to break the backbone of the insane killer.
Many arks are about tipping over with overload
of items denying others basic needs. Will there be
a flood to lift the ark till everywhere is cleansed?

21

Baba and Nene

(March 27, 2020)

Understandably, here and there
aren't the same measure

but what touches Baba* there
will inevitably befall Nene* here.

China is far from here
but what started there wouldn't end

until in America I witness firsthand
that the ogre isn't the hoax from afar.

There and here have collapsed into one space—
the playground and workplace of one experience.

The sun exercises suzerainty over every day
but today and tomorrow are bound to be different—

those born the same day, even twins, go separate ways;
each day carries its own fate on the forehead.

Baba is here, Nene is there.
We aren't the same but stranded in one season.

The road that runs through Ovu inevitably goes to Okpara;
what lands in Milan, Madrid, and London flies to New York!
Boiled or roasted, corn gets heated to be done.
There's convergence of far and near.

Undeniably, there and here
aren't the same measure

but what afflicts Nene in a distant world
inevitably comes to Baba in a fast-moving world.

*Baba and Nene are respectively Grandfather and Grandmother. Here, each represents both "we" and the other at different times in the community.

22

We All Value Our Lives

It takes an apocryphal tribulation
to freeze the hands abusing billions of non-human beings.
The trees have reprieve from those beheading them
to lounge in sleek furniture that attests to their status
but care not about the lives decimated for their comfort.
Locked down in their cruelty to others,
those who have perpetrated pain for ages
stripping the timber and character of trees
whose orchestra now plays with abandon.

Silence has built a novel ghost town
from the beehives of human abode
deferring everywhere to the invisible presence
that rattles its arrival with ambulances
and costumed medics; unbecoming stranger.
Super jets downed. Autos, trains and buses
stop puffing acrid fumes into the air
that bystanders inhale and suffocate from.

For sure, our non-human kinsfolks have respite
from human frenzy, a millennial madness;
they must be celebrating the demise of their abusers
so inhuman they have no regard for their neighbors.
Should the desperate humans recover their peace,
let this tribulation brand them with feelings for others,
the perennial victims of their outlandish disregard.
Let every being, human or non-human, thrive
in peace and reciprocity! We all value our lives.

23

Novel Fatalities

(March 28, 2020)

The monthly figures of gun fatalities dropped steeply
from the exponential increase of past bloodied decades.
Shooters have been paralyzed by the novel fear
of an invisible enemy on the loose in the boroughs
that cares not from what side of the city, west
or south, you have elected to plant your habitation.
Gender neutral, it seeks anyone to devour. Hide!

The monthly figures of shooting fatalities down to
an astonishing low; overtaken by coronavirus attacks
skyrocketing to nothing emergency wards ever saw.
In the land of the brave, an even braver alien warrior
sworn to bruising or knocking dead all on the way—
radicals and conservatives, straight and crooked folks
won't test the morbid temper of who sets IEDs around.

On scarce ventilators, those who own dozens of rifles;
others locked at home with a squadron's cache of ammo
and topmost officials of the international rifle association
unable to pull even one trigger against a brazen intruder!
When else in our lifetime could this paralysis have happened?
Hunters are themselves hunted! The brave, forgetting their
constitutional right, throw down gun and run blindly for life.

24

The Big Shame

Easily breaking through the network of NATO defenses
mocking the expensive toys shielding American airspace
defying rugged Russian air systems over Siberia

taunting the spiritual power of the Pope
damning invocations of African and Hindu gods
ridiculing the impotence of Greek and Roman gods

the littlest of things and without wings
and no claim to godhead and might
penetrates every type of armor invented

to humor the world that all this while
fanatically believes so much in its power
to keep off enemies it can think of

but not those that are not there for it
to scare off with thundering sounds
and prayers but astonish its knowledge

it is a big shame.

25

Air Fleet

This morning I take my daily walk
in a ghost town of a million entombed residents.
Overhead the raucous formations of birds
migrating from one region to another
each carrying the other along and aloft.
None will drop from the calibrated flight.

My ghost town of a million entombed residents—a land of
acknowledged noisy performers—startles with eerie silence.
To my right a lake and a flock of geese of no denomination
swim together immune from the lockdown in Ghost Town.
The wind blows, the wire grass and others dance
as if invigorated by the absence of human vagrants.
On trees carpenter bird and woodpecker beat their percussion
as the music of the orchestra on wings occupies the airspace.

Why do we wait to be cursed before allowing others to be happy?
This morning I take my daily walk
in my ghost town of a million entombed residents
and enjoy the company of other beings relishing their happiness.

26

Beyond My Expectation

(March 29, 2020)

I guessed all along that knowledge would kill all.
That was yesterday before today rolled its dice.
In the fierce rivalry for power and influence,
I had thought the world headed for self-destruction.
More lethal weapons got tested for accuracy.
Poisons without antidotes brewed in laboratories.
Witchcraft got approval of political archangels.

That was yesterday. Today the dice has rolled.
Who knows tomorrow? My guess is far from the point.
It is not yesterday's power that rules today;
we have not set ourselves on fire strong as the desires
to rob others to increase our wealth and leave them helpless.
The rich aren't doing well with encumbrances of materials—
the powerful are ready to relinquish might for good health.

At the rate we started, I thought we would kill ourselves
brewing more potent poisons to overwhelm others.
I feared accidental discharge would start the catastrophe
but lo, no accident or premeditated explosion.
Something else, not our knowledge and its hiccups, kills us;
something else, not the ingenuity for wealth or power.
I expected an explosion but met macabre silence.

27

What They Said

No power could keep the millennial congregation out, they said.
Today is Sunday and Dunamis Church* is closed for worship.
Folks said the traditional market never closes or gets postponed.
Agbarho's biweekly main market shut down on this market-day.

I now know established order cannot always remain sacrosanct.
I wondered when I didn't hear the call for evening prayers.
An unimagined catastrophe can happen and disrupt so effortlessly.
Those who see tomorrow know why they aren't easily surprised.

*Dunamis Church: a mega church on Airport Road, Abuja.

28

One Pod

A family cocoons in a pod and heals.
In Lagos, thanks to the clampdown,
children now see Daddy and Mommy at home.
There's no leaving for work at 5 am and only
back home after 10 pm with children gone to bed.
Daddy has not gone to the drinking spot or wherever
to squander his time and cash on pleasantries.
Mother has no reason for all the cultural meetings
that gave her alibi for her wanderings and dalliances.
The kids have no visitors and do not hang out with cultists.
They are all stuck to one another; one pod as cocoa
and kola nuts of the same tree thriving in a plantation.
With the cessation of pursuit of money and other businesses,
the members of the family have become one; stuck together.

29

Who Sleeps Well These Days?

(March 30, 2020)

Who sleeps well nowadays:
those already feverish and coughing with sore throats,
their contacts and relatives mindful of the jeopardy
or nurses and doctors whose gear is no miracle armor?

Who sleeps well nowadays:
those far away or near, if not sick in body
trembling to bed and through night sick in their minds
processing casualties as never before in wards and morgues?

Who sleeps well nowadays:
who, after the graphics of pain and panic in the news,
tales of folks dropping before testing or admission
and even pacified babies crying from the hysteria in the air?

Who sleeps well nowadays:
me, who sleepwalk to fumigate the long-evacuated village
of my childhood, quarantined in Grandpa's farm hut
where Papa all gray breathes steam and stays silent?

Who sleeps well nowadays:
those suffering the hubris of acquiring so much on earth
and thinking of Koro's arrival and its random attacks
or those consumed by plotting to make what they don't have?

Wailing dogs and cats stuttering messages they can't articulate,
the living stung by what they can't see or fathom
and in the dark without reflection or dawn at sight
who still sleeps well these days?

30

I Now Appreciate Better

I can now appreciate better
Mandela's twenty-seven years of incarceration.
He did not have the luxury
to self-isolate or quarantine for protection.
There were fascist guards watching him;
they passed him food through steel protectors
without luxury of opening his own refrigerator at will.
He had no set date of possible release;
unlike those to whom several months of lockdown
sound like the utmost sentence in judicial history.
Apartheid did not allow him to exercise his human rights,
unlike those who wave the Constitution to do others harm.
Pampered urchins downplay their perils
as they exaggerate what the world owes them.
Mandela tasted the tribulation of heroes;
we retreat into our homes for self-preservation.
I now appreciate better
Madiba's twenty-seven years of entombment
from which he rose to be the world's darling.

31

Other Perils

As we wage war against fatalities of doomsday infection,
other perils loom out there that we still need to beat back.
The earth writhes from inconsiderate abuse and convulses;
the provider suffers from the hands of its beneficiaries!
The forests more than half-gone, icy north and south no longer
fending off but succumbing to the scorching power of the sun;
no-one can tell what will become of the earth as we knew it
with all the changes that will not support the generosity to us—
we know we lose so much of what made us human to its abuse.
Factories, in the name of industrialization, puff carbon into
blackened lungs now ill-equipped to withstand a novel virus.
Many other battles compound our ability to win this world war.

32

Air Spaces

(March 31, 2020)

There's no certainty of things anymore;
as if earlier confidence changed our helplessness.

When will air spaces once no problem
for the frequent flyers to cross nations
reopen to meet distant ones waiting;
when for sure will the lockdown be rescinded
for travel to destinations of our hearts?

When shall social distancing go
for lovers apart to meet again
to compare experiences of separation
in diverse geographies that held them?

When will those like birds that flew out
to forage for food come back to nest?
When will the dark clouds clear
and lift off what oppresses our minds,
hearts, and souls day and night?

There's no certainty of things anymore;
as if past bravado covered our weakness.

33

Prayers

At the back of the mind
religious or not, believer or not
spiritual, secular, or not
one of the multiple thoughts
conspicuous or unobtrusive
but there a fixed presence:
the prayer, invocation, or
something else by whatever name
Let this plague pass me by!
silently intoned and repeated
for efficacy and kept sacred
when we are trembling because
others caught the terrible thing.

34

Tomorrow After Tomorrow

When what we thought impossible
happened, we swallowed our words.
At the rate of being proved wrong,
who says that someday the hen
wouldn't grow teeth and smile at us?
Who knows the power of tomorrow
after tomorrow in transforming things?
So, who lives long discovers what life is:
the impossible becomes possible
as yesterday's unreal becomes so real.

35

Spreading Hysteria

I have just called to check on my friend
living where the CDC* says is a hotspot.

"I am not afraid of coronavirus," he told me,
and continued: "I am losing my eyesight fast.
I live alone in my apartment. What's worse
than living alone and blind?" Not coronavirus
sowing seeds of panic everywhere in the world.

I wonder why contracting the affliction reaping
a macabre harvest where it has not planted life
pales before a blind lone man in an apartment.
I would pray for him to have fortitude of mind.
I hope he wouldn't curse me for spreading hysteria.

*CDC: Center for Disease Control, Atlanta, GA

36

To One, Distant

(April 1, 2020)

Now there's no handshake, no hugging
bodies compulsorily apart

I send this bouquet of songs
through a love-sanitized network

in which distant and nearby places
merge into a correspondence of oneness

so that tomorrow will more than redeem
today's depressing denials.

37

Epiphany

When I think of
the possibility of the impossible
the reality of the unreal
universal acceptance of individual denials
the cheapness of the expensive
the pettiness of the big power
the shallowness of the abysmal
the darkness of the clearest tomorrow
the crookedness of the erect mindset

I am simultaneously contemplating
what the world would become after
the devastation of such a little one
combating hand-to-hand the distant marauder
a Milanese model delivers a monster
backward folks ferry the world across a dead sea
the wager loses all the wages from exploitation
the coroner convalesces from convulsion
a death sentence commutes to a six-month lockdown
and life returns after rigor mortis.

38

Chloroquine

If the news turns true that the weapon of the weak
outperforms the sophisticated arsenal of the powerful,
then it's a real new world that has arrived.

If the evidence proves true that the antimalarial medication
can cure the affliction of the novel coronavirus,
then power rotates at its chosen time.

If confirmed that what brings down malaria in Africa
has become the developed world's miracle drug,
then we should not look down on challenged folks.

If the conquerors of history desperately seek the assistance
of those who have not yet recovered from downtrodden bruises,
let no-one boast of tomorrow's tallies of accomplishments.

And if Africans reeled for centuries from malaria
to save the rest of the world with their regular treatment,
let everybody live together in mutual respect.

39

Ways of Dying

Where folks have been left on their own
in doldrums to wage war against legions of denials
as one government after another made fools of them,
why should governors and president choose for them
their way of dying?

The people, used to surviving against odds,
would rather roll the dice again
with the hope of beating back a weaker aggressor,
their term for a feverish infection however choking,
than locked down without cash and food
and exposed to the cruel pangs of hunger
that would inevitably drain life out of them.

The public would rather fight in their markets
than famished and quartered at home for the sacrifice
they know their chieftains would as usual escape.
They want to make the choice, not rigged into dying,
to fight and come out alive bruised all over
rather than cooped where hunger would pick their flesh
and leave skeletons in their unlit and hot homes.

They want to be outside on their feet fighting back
than sit at home waiting to be mauled by their principal foe;
they would rather fight the adversity of their choice.
Why should chieftains choose for others, harried from all sides,
their preferred way of dying?

40

Social Distancing

The lords are suspending their house helps
after stockpiling their pantries and vacant rooms.
Drivers have become dispensable threats to car-owners
because they come from Mararaba*, an inflammable hotspot.
The patriarchs are not taking in new brides
until they are a hundred percent sure of a negative public.
And kings are refusing tributes for the time being
after building a fortune from resources of their subjects.
They are all practicing social distancing indeed!

*Mararaba: a small crowded town in Nasarawa State, Nigeria, that is the home of
many junior workers in Abuja, Nigeria

41

Tomorrow for Others

Tomorrow will come with or without us
but the sun will still rise and set;
the rain will fall its measure of moisture
and the season's plants flaunt their flowers
without concern for afflictions on the loose,
without worries for testing positive or negative
and unmindful of lockdowns and quarantines
that have no place in their cycle. They follow
their pathways without a government order.

42

A Net Over Italy

(April 3, 2020)

Death threw a vast net over Italy
and the land flares with grief.
The eerie music possesses so many
to dance to its rhythm out of this world.
Nowhere does a single traveler beyond
leave with such company; an exodus.

The daily tally benumbs the mind.
No church bells toll for the celebrants
thrown into cold trucks to God-knows—
nobody sees this wave and not shiver.
The boats to afterlife a dizzying dirge
of shadows not prepared for departure
but forced to leave empty-handed.

No memorial because there's no space;
no tribute beyond a bowed head;
no one close by to wail and cheer up
the lone voyager and the silent cortege
into earth or fire to consume wholesale.

The rains that fall across the land roll
tears down brows of those left behind;
the sun that shines over the land
prepares folks to be easy preys.
There death has reaped a number;
the soil choked by the staple of bones.
The republic has become a boneyard
where day dawns with disbelief.

43

Don't Bother!

Nobody should tell me to leave him alone.
I won't bother to go even if he invites me.
I have chosen to retire to a hermitage, an un
discovered place off radar from this world.
I won't bring anybody in. Covid-19 forbids me.
My social instincts have become counterproductive
to thrive in a new world without assemblies.
I won't complain of self-isolation, nor will I
rant about rights because of government lockdown.
It is high time we deferred to the other side—
this aloneness that some have been demanding;
time for the majority to live on the minority's staple.
Nobody should tell me to stay away from him.
Let him not bother. I won't go there even if invited.

44

The Roads Are Clear

It's not a matter of what I want.
Also not a matter of what you desire.
I am alone;
the streets are lonely.
You must be alone too
and the roads are clear of traffic.
The time is there for a tryst:
morning through afternoon to evening
and often the weather cools as if to coax us.
Our minds are desirous
but that's not enough
to go through open spaces,
to use the abundance of free time
and to meet because we want to hug.
There's a new correspondence:
helplessness before opportunities.
It's not a matter of what anybody wants,
since we are caught up in this world
that has flipped in just a few months
and we are seeking a new bearing
as we attempt to reclaim old love.

45

The Mind of This Season

(April 4, 2020)

One counts but to no finitude.
There's promise but no assurance—
nobody tells me when the dark
but dehydrated clouds would lift
much as one knows of every season
however stubborn and harsh it settles
will go whether it came slowly or suddenly.

It is a matter of time for every season
but I cannot count to its infinitude.
There's a monstrosity of the normal
and it slips through despite communal efforts
and the best of mental calculations;
expectations of respecting normalcy.

The littlest of a monster on the loose,
a diabolic presence across the globe
mauls day and night with impunity
as humans counter the sickening spells
with their available medicinal resources.
But when will the fiercely dark clouds lift?

Who knows the mind of this season?
Maybe tomorrow but surely not today—
I cannot count to the season's finitude;
its stubbornness and monstrosity openly
defy my counting craft of a season's lifetime.

46

Witness History

It does not only catch our attention
in its movement, defying blockades
and mojos of mystical warriors
and carried, ferried and flown everywhere
but also gets the world fixated to its fixtures.

We all witness its invisible presence.
It shakes the world to its seams
and whether monster or mass murderer,
we witness its indelible trail of havoc.
It is making history. We all witness it.

It catches attention. It makes us change
habits, revise our reasoning on small ones.
It redefines power and where it thrives
unshaken by the mightiest of tsunamis.
It trashes wealth and confirms life's vagaries.

The dirge in its wake still streams live
on all media, digital or town-crier's gong.
It does not only catch every attention
with its collaterals but also makes us
witness history in its stark unfolding.

47

The Invisible One at Large

My daughter wheels herself away
once the network news begins
to reel out the ponderous toll—
thousands of casualties from forays
of the invisible but intimidating foe.
I try to change the channel elsewhere
to keep out of sight the dreaded one
but station after station takes me
to the same dread that defies damning.
And in my sleep the fresh images
of sick and dead streaming, I walk
backwards and wake in cold sweat.
The invisible one chases me everywhere
to jump out of my foothold to seek refuge
where it is already dug in and directing
its macabre warfare to cleanse the earth.
And there's no room again for anything else
but Covid-19; the invisible one on the loose.

48

They Prepared the Earth for Its Coming

(April 5, 2020)

They prepared the earth for its coming
and once arrived, it turned into something else:
apocalyptic figure without face, footprints, and
voice exercising absolute power of invisibility.
Its human consumption appalls even the earth.

They prepared the world for its coming
and for supreme victory over fun lovers;
they elected nincompoops as presidents
in strategic nations to be worthy allies
to arm it with supernatural precision.

They prepared everywhere for its rise
to stardom and epic stature. There were
enough doubters to catch by surprise.
A few wise ones around know discretion
in retreating out of its way into solitude.

They prepared the earth for its harangues—
the Facebook community crowned it
the king of all monsters and once viral
it got into its microscopic head to spread;
then on there was nowhere out of its reach.

They availed planes and ships, buses and trains,
and even staged Mardi Gras to herald its coming.
Once it arrived, it spread its infectious craft.
Upon all invisible, it made absolute fools
of knowledgeable people blind and clueless.
The earth is coming to know what it prepared
for—the confusion of a world-changing crisis.
It was so effective fulfilling its secret mission
because the earth and folks prepared for its coming
and once here it has been another matter altogether.

49

Fattening the Beast for Sacrifice

In some cultures, they fatten the animal
they want to use for sacrifice. Outsiders
had thought it barbaric and so bizarre.
Then a strong ill wind blew in and to
prevent the collapse of material structures,
those outsiders now give employment
to folks to save the huge Stock Market
in the season of Covid-19 that's at large.
Naïve ones came out only to fall casualties;
their savings to be inherited by others.
There are frantic calls to coax workers
from safe isolation for high compensations
only for the exposed groomed ones
to be mauled by the invisible monster.
The rite has become global: fatten the beast
and use it for sacrifice to prolong your life!

50

Millennial Trepidations

(April 6, 2020)

This millennium arrived with trepidations of its crossover—
what held the world together would let go for God-knows-
what type of disjuncture and a re-calibration afterwards.
Educated fortunetellers predicted computer crashes
that would be so calamitous and costly as wiping out all
security, wealth and years of knowledge; a global Armageddon.
I did not fall for the expensive hoax or trending superstitions—
I was in the air the very night of the crossover that many
expected the stroke of midnight to be the end of the world.

But not long into the century after the confidence that
the technology of the global community's collaboration
would save all, came this unraveling of a pandemic.
What we expected and feared—the millennial crossover—
came and passed; our frantic preparations only alarm teasers.
Now strutting to the music of affluence and power, confident
that nothing can stop us and no prediction of a crossover,
we plunge head-on into the morbid mess of Covid-19!
It's when unprepared that the monster arrives with vengeance.

51

Keeping Safe

It matters not what I fancy to look fashionable
but what I need to survive this infectious season—
not the shibboleth of high culture but protective gears.
Milan, Paris, and NYC closed shop for the spring;
the models and their catwalks with sedate judges
and cheering spectators faded to a bygone era.
Beauty's delicacy that possessed the eyes of yesterday
has today been sidelined for utilitarian desires.
The face swath suffocates but shields me and that's
why when I take my morning walk, I lose freedom as
I knew it. Pursuing fancy has turned into an infraction.
All of a sudden to be safe I hop into specific spaces
in the tic-tac-toe landscape of today's dos and don'ts.
It's not what I fancy but all to keep safe. I suspend
the fashion I will don for a victory parade someday
for this armor in today's raging warfront of Covid-19.

52

New Communion

Social distancing and self-isolation have separated us—
we are farther than triple arm's length from each other
mulling over the dire consequences of proximity;
the incalculable harm of leaning on one another, shaking
hands and embracing as one world of love and solidarity.

We may be farther apart in our retreats to be safe, since
it's a hazard to walk to a neighbor's or pay a distant visit
but the volume of phone calls to check on you, the flood
gate of email and Facebook messages, greetings, and
goodwill thoughts the other person doesn't know about
all more than make up for the physicality of proximity.

The communion has changed from sitting round a table
and indulging in bread and wine to the close company
of heart and mind, a bonding that wraps us together.
There's something sacred in being so close when apart
that makes this new relationship such a fulfilling wonder.

53

The Daring Game

(April 7, 2020)

Who is daring whom on what these days?
I dare you sail a softwood raft across the Atlantic.
I dare you fly non-stop from Reykjavik to the South Pole.

I dare you suspend the Olympics from breaking its own records.
I dare you play the Europa championship finals in a subterranean stadium.
I dare you perform the quietest Calypso carnival in summer West London.

Let me dare you more these days that need heroic acts.
Command the ocean waves to crest on the moon!
Disorient the marauding one to suffer a major dislocation!

I dare you to dare the un-dare-able:
transform Covid-19 into a hulk jogging in Central Park*
so that we keep distant from the terror or even assassinate it!

Daring is human, I hear folks say in pursuit of their desires.
I dare you to slaughter the centaur of the new century
and display its invisible head on HD images for the world to see!

*Central Park: in New York.

54

Narrow Escapes

My first cousin lived a week on a ventilator in New York where
my colleague's only child fought to remain alive in his deadly ward.
My friend's family racked with his son's positive test in Potomac
and another kinsman just came out of a respirator in Charlotte.
Covid-19 has breached my circle of close relatives and friends.
Who says this litany of survivors does not hit me enough
with them escaping narrowly than almost caught by a sliver?

55

A Tale of Two Patients

In Abuja a superhuman man hunkered in a rock cave
contracts what has infected over a million folks in the globe
and they fly him to an unknown destination for treatment.
Since nobody knows his whereabouts—Lagos, Havana, or hell,
rumors proliferate of his disappearance from primetime circulation.

In London the chief minister latches to oxygen at St. Thomas's
 already tested by a relentless flood of severe cases.
There are daily briefings to demystify his stature as superman;
only a fighter pulling together all his resources to overcome
his people's enemy that he took as a personal challenge to die for.

The same virus infects Abuja's big man and London's front man.
Why the hiding of who's about to die whose nakedness
will not be within his power to cover when laid to rest?
Those who live in darkness suffocate from rumors of evil wishes
and those who are transparent heal from prayers of goodwill.

56

Morning Call

(April 8, 2020)

So assuring this daily morning call
that one looks up to—
as Grandpa looked up to and welcomed
with soulful song the falcon's
yearly appearance on the horizon
that kept him into a centenarian.

This daily morning call
keeps the night shorter than normal,
sleep deeper than one can fathom
and the body infused with youthful zest
despite the benumbing statistics,
despite the dirge-filled but still air
and despite lurid images of late-night television.

This spontaneous morning call wakes me
to look up to life's sustaining side
to prime myself to laughter
in the night of streaming tears
to expect ecstasy
in the midst of fear.

Like when young I looked up to
the cattle egret in its yearly return
we knew another green season had come
and we piled them into decades of plenty,
this morning call is an elixir
despite the viral contagion and its havoc.

I look up to this morning call
to inhale uplifting sweet words
and to exhale the carbon
of infecting particles.
I am going to call now

looking up to the communion
that fortifies me for another day.

57

Leopard in a Cornfield

The stillness of night
a crepuscular day
leopard in a cornfield
the leaping of a year
out of the void of eons
so sudden and without fear
or favor out of the spirit world
a gnome banished from there
to seek a home where it doesn't
belong but roams until
it spends itself drowned
in the diurnal dirges
of the alien invasion
belying the stillness of night
and a crepuscular day
a leopard in a cornfield
the surreal handiwork of one
banished from another world
blazing an invisible trail
of downtrodden and lords
bound hands and feet struggling
to untie the knot that's
a riddle of what tomorrow holds
on a still night
and a crepuscular day
with a leopard in the cornfield.

58

There's Other News

(April 9, 2020)

Other than the haunting casualties of coronavirus,
other than muted celebrations of recovery
in the face of a heavy toll,
other than debates about the role of destiny
in all this—many unscathed, others dying or narrowly
escaping the virulent skirmishes and battles
in the pandemic war of 2019-2020—

there's other news. Individually, the milestone
of a birthday, the failure in a contest that would have been
great and for which a friend consoles you for your past glories
and unexpectedly a friend's daughter wins a scholarship.

Statistics of road accidents down to almost zero;
the same of kidnapping and armed robberies.
Mass shootings seem to be last century's blemish,
as gangs call a truce to distribute food to vulnerable elderly.
So much transformation that marks out the season
a turning point from the barbarisms that bedeviled us.

There's other news not breaking as Covid-19's.
For many, the coming of downpours
to douse the intolerable heat of the tropics;
in some lands despite the lockdown
they cannot resist the seduction of cherry blossoms
and where the viral decimation astounds
it's the first warm days that turn things
to spring to life.

Other than Covid-19, there's other news;
good or bad but something different
and also worth remembering this very year.

59

For the Other's Sake

Bad dreams only at night wouldn't hurt so much
if daylight was not a continuation of worse dreams
and day wouldn't be unbearable if one looked
up to night for relief it hasn't in its novel holocaust.

With neither night nor day free of torture,
there's nowhere else to escape to
outside of the known world that is life's
only sovereign state; the earth.

Reaching others fills day and night with words
to calm nerves; balm to the sore hearts we suffer
from the rack of Covid-19. We all share the helpless
plight across distances without movement.

We then wake to turn into a caring community,
fall asleep and in place of nightmares sweet dreams
and that's how to even out night and day
and save ourselves for the other's sake.

60

The Literature of Covid-19

(April 10, 2020)

In literature Covid-19 is only a trope—
what you prepare for isn't what you always get;
the knotty question that deprives a student of a perfect score;
the lacking omniscience that prevents the doctor from being God.

The whole thing is a potpourri of systems being tested—
the imperfections now beautiful, the social realism
of underlying factors affecting success or failure rates.
There's the context to contend with in counter-discourse.

Literature defines all happenings existentially—
the comedy or tragedy on the stage; good and bad.
Don't blame it on literature that got it right—so ironical;
Covid-19 is only a trope for life: good and bad things happen.

61

Tall Expectations

I had thought amidst its rage
Covid-19 would rearrange the order of things
as we had not known it:
bring the rich to the same level as the poor,
the able-bodied accepting the equality of the disabled;
social distancing would turn people used to huddling
to keep off their boisterous crowds to be loners,
and old dos become new don'ts and old don'ts new dos

but despite the consuming rage
it has not yet devoured racism but magnified it
not only in the color codes of lopsided casualties
and the colonialist thought of testing vaccines among
those who suffered the least toll of the pandemic*
but also the heinous insult of whose soil bred the virus
assaulting Africans in their midst for excuses. . .

I had thought amidst its rage
the scourge would convert all into novel human beings—
my expectations of the order as high as Kilimanjaro—
but the cleansing of evil remains mostly undone.
Even before it peaks and leaves folks alone,
Covid-19 may re-arrange the order of some things
but my fear is that survivors of this holocaust
returning to unleash grimmest inhumanity on others.

*Two French scientists, Jean Paul Mira and Camille Locht, had suggested to the world's dismay that the anti-coronavirus vaccine should be first tested in Africa where the infection and death rates then were far lower than Europe's.

62

Ode to Solitude

For the first time I am alone—
I don't want anybody near me.
I look closely at myself and find my first gray hairs.
I discover a birthmark, not a scar, on my right hand
I have been working with for tough decades.
I review my life and how not to do things
that need to be turned around for good—
keep silent and enjoy the music within;
an ear-stopper against noise that brings headaches.
I discover that without my trifocals I see farther.
I hear the sound of silence and its clear message.
I feel the divine—enough time to commit to the invisible.
I prosecute and defend me in a court where I am the jury.
I am not worried as I am able to do what I used to dismiss—
fast effortlessly as the day passes without my knowing.
I do not need to make money to be happy;
I am happy without competition for advantage over others.
This quarantine has liberated me from self-bondage,
and for the first time I am alone and so happy.

63

Lessons from Self-isolation

I am learning so much in my self-isolation.

One fright cannot scare off all recalcitrant
aggressors from despoiling the earth;
one battle may not win the war of attrition.

One pandemic cannot cleanse the earth
of bad habits—if it could, there would
be no racism, no robbery or injustice;
one tsunami cannot wash off all the dirt—
if it could, garbage wouldn't be choking.

One blaze will not rid the world of all
inflammables and vermin—if it does,
there will be no toll from arson or rage.
One dismal season would not depopulate
the earth; if it could populations wouldn't
be spiking to clog every space available.
No one virus can change the world's history;
if it does old practices won't be hanging on.

I am learning so much in this self-isolation.

64

Healing

(April 11, 2020)

In addition to the circle of regulars,
yes, those whose messages at dawn
have become tonic to the blood, fresh
draughts of sustaining therapeutic air
and with whom you are locked in heartbeat,

there are those like stragglers who advance
from the dark for recognition—they pray
for you as they themselves need prayers.
Then, those who had broken off over nothing
and for self-healing seek peace and the message
out of nowhere so as to be counted among loved ones.

Places of worship are closed to observe social distancing
but faith in others couldn't be stronger—
the human invocation of the divine in one another
and the longing to clean the in-house to be spritely
to summon one's mental resources to survive.

So, there are two kinds of messages, regular
and unexpected in the season of reconciliation
of human kinsfolks struggling to be safe
stretch their distant hands not only to lift
but be also lifted out of the grip of Covid-19.

65

You Keep Watch Over Us

(for Dr. Tedros Ghebreyesus*)

To many
it's only their county or local government
it's only their state or province
it's only their nation or kingdom
it's only their ethnic group or race
it's only their fellow worshippers
it's only their class, party, or bedfellows

and they are shortsighted—
they see only the immediate surrounding
they do not see beyond the mayoralty
they do not see beyond the state or province
they do not see beyond the nation or kingdom
they do not see beyond the race or religion
they do not see beyond whom they are comfortable with

but you have the world as your circle
not constricted to a parochial constituency
but the entire humankind—
everybody is your relative
and you are everyone's keeper
irrespective of so many diminishing themselves
and we all still sleep as well as can be
because you are watching over us
with the semi-divine eyes of WHO.

*Dr. Tedros Adhanom Ghebreyesus, an Ethiopian, is Director-General of the
World Health Organization (WHO). He is the apparent leader of the world in
the fight against COVID-19.

66

Fools

(April 12, 2020)

There have been those so daring
that they became fools to pity:
a state regulatory official having a haircut
in the capital's South side's only open salon;
a celebrity throwing a party for a partner's
birthday in a gated estate under curfew;
a minister driving a long distance with a pass
to change homes when in charge of lockdown;
and a king taking a contingent of consorts to holiday
in the North Pole far from his unravelling kingdom.

They were all caught as they didn't expect,
thanks to the irreverent eyes of social media,
and paraded on network news for breaking
the law and exposing others to Covid-19.
It takes only a fool not to admit being a fool
when caught doing wrong and exposed to
the infamy of self-centeredness that imperils
not only those they love but not apologizing
for being out of step with the trembling world.
They were too daring to hide under public glare.

67

Easter Sunday

It's Easter Sunday.
Services canceled
because of social distancing
but inexorably the day passes
with twenty-four evenly-paced strides.
Easter passes without fanfare.
Covid-19 is such a terror
but it cannot scare time to a standstill.
Rather, it rages on, its dust
and litters materials for history.

68

Of God and Archangels

(April 13, 2020)

To the patient
the doctor must be God
and nurses and other health workers archangels.
They save.
But when any of them gets stricken
and becomes a patient
doctor or assistant loses the godhead
to become a mere mortal
who in the dire battle
at the great crossroads
could go either way—
take the forlorn road into another world
or retreat to the known, whatever its foreboding.
To the patient
the doctor must be God.

69

We Are All Casualties

We knew people ambulanced to hospital
but did not return,
we know who returned on their own feet
but stunned to silence by their vulnerability;
we know those whose relatives or friends
either lost or won their personal battles.
All the while we have stayed at home.
It is not that distant despite social distancing—
those who grieve for the dead,
those who participate in muted celebrations,
and those who suffer enervating trepidations
from the fatalities trucked to mass graves
and the losses no words can convey.
Dead, positive, or negative
we are all casualties of Covid-19.

70

We Shall Overcome

The coronavirus cannot bring down the sky,
it cannot pull down Mount Kilimanjaro;
it cannot drain the Atlantic Ocean of its salt.
It rages past forests but uproots no single iroko,
it passes the Tiber River and doesn't affect its flow;
it cannot arrest any typhoon or Southern tornadoes.
It can't rescue Nigeria from corruption's stranglehold.

It has the power of a mudslide
that buries quite a number and is done;
it is like a cataclysmic earthquake
that devastates populations but only a phenomenon;
it depopulates disproportionately
but cannot decimate the world into a wasteland.

It is not bending the world to break its backbone,
it is not flushing out all the undesirables
that make different kinds of humans inhuman;
it is a terror but not that powerful
to remove sit-tight leaders crushing their people.

Folks will thrust their fists into the air
and prepare for the next battle
in the perennial war of human existence.
Enough to win one battle and recuperate
from wounds and arm for the future.
We shall overcome Covid-19!

71

So Many Things We Can Do Without

(April 14, 2020)

So many things we can do without
and still be fine—

in place of loud prayers
silent supplications that go straight to the divine.
Of what use are intercessors
in days of abundance of time in our hands?
Of what use are servants
that come and go and we can't trust with our lives?
Of what use are needless gestures
or homage to over-demanding gods of our making?

So many things we can do without
and still be fine—

pursuing capital as if the end-all of life,
making love as if love apart isn't so beautiful,
seeking every attention as if smiling lavishly
would take a selfie with Covid-19 in person;
not slowing down and ever racing ahead
as if not shortening life by shortcuts.
For once, there are many things on hold
that make life a river's smooth flow to the sea.
Good to stop and exhale; even cast off old skin.

So many things we can do without
and still be very fine.

72

An American Soliloquy

(April 15, 2020)

Maybe we were stupid, maybe not
in the blind spot of our intelligence,
in the assured language of our indulgence
bound by our exceptional destiny
that we were certainly not Chinese or others
whose diet of weird foodstuffs started it all.

Since the epicenter was thousands of miles away,
we regaled in bars and stadia for safety.
When the contagion flared in familiar Europe
where our immigrant ancestors lived glorious lives,
we still didn't know those far and near shared one planet
and breathed the same air, cold or warm but one mass.

And now it strikes here harder than elsewhere,
we realize we all die: Chinese, others, and us.
Maybe we were stupid; maybe just human
believing only in our intelligence and doubting others.
We lived in the blind spot of our turtle island shield.
The coronavirus made us really human like others.

73

In Memoriam

(for Mrs. Phoebe Ogundipe, who passed on at 92 of natural causes in Charlotte, NC)

This is not a good time to die.
From thronged wards, so many rolled out
into trucks for incineration or dumped into vast pits.

I have heard of who deserves celebrations
for long life that qualifies her to be a great ancestor;
the passing for which a cortege leads to afterlife—
the sort that deserves a pyramid over her.
Many have died without even a muted farewell.

Ma Ogundipe has gone to join the ancestors
but there's no space in social distancing to send her off;
no songs and dances to escort her away in a lockdown;
no gathering of lineage and well-wishers to acknowledge her,
no staccato of gunshots as reminder of her ninety-two years.

There's never been any good time to die.
Better not die from or during a raging pandemic,
better not die when the world hangs in the balance;
better to die after cessation of the global logjam.
It's really never good to die at any time.

You have been buried but remain unburied.
Let this dirge accompany you beyond.
Still, this is not a good time to die.

74

Flat and Tasteless

Put them together—

Indian spices
Nigerian peppers
Jamaican curry and Tabasco
world-class aphrodisiacs
thyme, clove, cumin
and lemon grass—

for a fisherman's pepper soup
which unfortunately for the palate
in the mouth of a virus victim
all flavors turn the same:
flat and tasteless!

75

Fresh Casualties

(after watching news of police shootings in Nigerian streets to enforce the lock-
down to curb the spread of Covid-19)

(April 16, 2020)

Between the government and the people
there's no meeting of minds—
the police kill more than coronavirus;
more die from robbers in their homes than viral infections;
the bureaucrats in front seats hoard rice and flour
their government promised the people to stay indoors;
the citizens are dying, the deaf president is snoring.

Between the government and the people
there's no meeting of minds—
hunger is mauling those locked down; casualties
from the virus still not visible in their midst,
who blames them for wanting to break out
to confront a lethal enemy to fend for themselves
than sit at home and be picked clean; skeletons?

The government is tackling down the people,
handicapping them with orders that bind with ropes—
they can't be free in their own land; they believe
those who rule them hate them worse than any virus.
The people are resistance fighters, falling, rising, falling
and hoping someday to overcome not only coronavirus
and hunger but also the monsters called leaders.

76

Nobody Knows

(April 17, 2020)

Nobody knows when
lovers apart will fly into each other's arms,
separated children and parents will have their family reunion,
or students and teachers interact within a physical classroom.

Nobody knows when the lockdown will lift
not by president or governor but by intuition;
when the habit of distancing will not inhibit close contact,
and our nature to again be good lovers, parents, and teachers.

We are waiting for when the birds flying out of their nests
into the horizon will be back with fresh vision and songs,
when the lioness will leave her separate den in the veldt
for a field day with the lion seeking her for companionship.

The sun bird is crying for its mate beyond its call's reach,
the family tree needs roots, trunk, branches, and leaves for its height;
the students clamor to interact in the building with their teacher
but when? Nobody knows when despite this long waiting.

The nest is safe in a storm but it has no window;
staying indoors is safe but closes outdoors of adventure.
Carefulness saves but spontaneity liberates from rigidity
and distancing however great is still antisocial behavior.

When shall we heal fully after being discharged,
when shall our tears again become medals of happiness;
when shall the dark clouds lift to spread salt in the sun,
when shall we go outdoors to dance after shutting indoors?

77

The Estrangement

My last-born has not shown up at home for several weeks.
He would normally spend Saturday to Monday here
but now has to distance from me, mom, and sister—
all three of us in a vulnerable category sheltering alone —
since he works in the hospital and we don't want him
to bring anything from there to infect us here indoors.
Mommy as Mother Hen is restive because of her last-born
and I tell her: "We're separating to be all well and together later."
I can see in the long mother-son's phone conversation a longing
to cluster but which common sense rejects for this estrangement.
I notice his sister mulling over their missing banter and laughter.
The father-son rivalry played out in weekly table tennis contests
on hold. I fear I won't grow old in the lockdown as not to
always narrowly win and he narrowly lose after this is over.
My son has not shown up at home for weeks. I know not when.

78

When a Virus is a Liberator

(April 18, 2020)

There's a death in the land.
The vulture dies and the streets burst
into dance and ululation; a sad but happy tale.
When the media reports the death of a high one
and the streets pour out with songs of jubilation,
folks wielding power should re-examine their lives.
Rulers should re-examine their exceptional lives
when the people celebrate a virus as their liberator.

Who announces the death of one to the world
and for which there's dance and ululation,
what's in his mind when alone from his task?
Rulers and their spokesmen should reflect daily
on what awaits them; the jeers or cheers ahead.
Nobody knows that power would give them up
until they die packaged in a box and thrown
into a pit that hyenas will ransack for bones.

There's death in the land
and nobody weeps for a dead vulture
but those of the same kind or clan are stung to silence
as folks welcome the news with dance and ululation.
Rulers and their allies who hear of this death
should re-examine their lives and ponder over power
lest someday the public will celebrate their death as vultures.
They must ponder on what happens when a vulture dies
and people sing to salute their invisible liberator.

79

Global Virus, Global Relief

I once maligned Facebook and its global kind
and still mistrust their exhibitionist character
but I now see the good role they play among us.
I now know that there's good or bad in everything
and that's enough reason for its existence.

"Facebook keeps me company all the time."
"WhatsApp is my lifeline in total isolation."
"Instagram and Twitter save me from lockdown."
Chatting, video calls, and postings of groups are
tools technology uses to mock social distancing.

What goes viral saves from viral affliction itself,
what spreads exponentially eventually covers the world;
the global village that one mistrusts at one's peril.
Yes, the global fuels Covid-19; it is global in reach
but global tools have become great stress relievers.

There's good or bad in everything we have to live with.
What would life be like today without Facebook,
WhatsApp, Instagram, and other shared communities?
More than lonesome, boring, and depressing; hence global
tools to cope with the global challenge of the coronavirus.

80

State of the World

The UNO has gone AWOL.
NATO has gone AWOL.
Empire builders of the past hit the hardest.
Italy, Spain, France and others count their losses in bones;
everyone to one's government. Live or die a citizen!
Britain nearly tipped over a precipice but for luck.
America falls from first to last in preparedness;
nobody now looks up to New York or Hollywood.

Africa again suffering from Europe's greed—
infected by foreign airlines to prop their markets.
Only God drives flies away from a tailless cow.
China's bats, not Africa's rats, the source of trouble
as the anthill nation proves a rabid racist all through.
Ecuador exposes South America to shocking disorder
as Brazil braces for the morbid consequence of denial.

The afflicted and casualties are numbered by nationality.
No superpower, rich or poor nation, spared the challenge.
Even the UNO has gone AWOL.
What a small world of only patriots and nationalists
without humanists caring for all!

81

Safety

(April 19, 2020)

We used to feel safe collectively;
hence we banded together against perils
but Covid-19 has altered that calculation of numbers—
safety today comes from keeping quite a distance away.

So no one is surprised at a group with some positives
disbanded and taken to quarantine to avert implosion;
no one surprised at the new formations of defense—
six to eight feet apart; far beyond earshot of others

without fear of the line or circle being breached,
without concern for others but only one's survival
in a war where Discharged is not dishonorable
but something to celebrate; one's triumph over odds.

Those together instead of being shielded by numbers
expose themselves to suffering terrible casualties;
everybody conscripted as a foot soldier of social distancing
or a self-decorated officer in isolation of a fantasy brigade.

Nobody ever thought of when fighting singly
would be more effective than as an army massed together
but Covid-19 has altered that calculation of numbers.
Safety lies in keeping far away from all forms of gathering.

82

Nobody Dies Alone

Nobody dies alone.
On the surface, one dies in the ward
but in that one death
a family of parents, children, and relatives,
friends, colleagues, and neighbors.

Every statistic is a loss
to a circle the person once belonged.
When the tree falls, it falls with trunk, branches, and
leaves. Its echo reaches birds, animals, and humans.
Even the hermit has relatives unknown to the recluse.

Nobody dies alone.
Many die with the deceased
however lonely the experience of dying
and the passage. The dead leave memories
behind with someone or many dying with them.

83

At Some Time

At some time
hope wrestles with fear
life seeks advantage over death
self-isolation provides company
social distancing brings proximity

more reflection in who has had
no time or thought of thinking
about things—setting up a shrine
creating one's God, not a pastor's
one's own prosecutor or defense
acquitting to live a positive life
or granting clemency in one's jury
stretching one's hand through the void
of unknown presences without voice
to grasp an angel of one's fancy
to refuge in an impregnable fort.

At some time
hope overcomes fear
life conquers death in the pyrrhic
victory of a battle in a war
bound to end only one way
which for now
we pretend not to know.

84

The Day's Report

(April 20, 2020)

All these frenetic months into the raging affliction,
World War III by a social media name,
there's not much to report than before.

A survivor had double resurrection in not only recovery
from the attack but also came out of a life of isolation—
his phone call not only astounded but also filled me
with the joy of the prodigal son who found his way home;
thanks to Covid-19 impelling its patients to self-reflect.

The world flares with controversy as always
between safety and capital. Among the impoverished
of the South, bold defiance against any form of lockdown;
in the North, where poverty is an eyesore among the affluent,
dollar barons incite workers with incentives to take fatal risks.

The world has not moved the dial from antiquated biases—
racism more rabid, tales from Guangzhou* chill every African
to rethink about those who enjoy hospitality in their homeland;
those who carry the cross on their forehead a heartless bunch;
and those that history disabled still unable to stand on their feet.

Yes, there's self-isolation, a journey inwards, but a virus
cannot cleanse the world of the wrongs for which prejudice
and exploitation had left their victims scarred for centuries.
Today, several hectic months into the raging World War III,
more fatalities in the opulent half of the world, the rest unsure.
One would want cheerful news to report as afflictions rage on.

---

*Guangzhou: a province in China where there were racist attacks on Africans
during the Covid-19 period.

85

Grandma's Injunction a Half Century Ago

My Grandma's injunction a half century ago
comes to pass in this very menacing season.
She admonished me to keep distant from evil
and not trust anyone incarnating or carrying it.
She made me suspect relatives, friends, and strangers.
I wondered about the extent I could distance myself,
the level of distrust of others if I was to be safe
and free. I feared for my life at home and outside.

Now the novel coronavirus leaves me at this point
with no safer alternative than social distancing.
This must be the evil talked about a half century ago;
averting contact with those contaminated with contagion.
My Grandma knew her stuff; her one day is a lifetime.
When she told me what the elder tells a child in the morning
will come to pass before nightfall, she foresaw this coming.
I am now keeping distant from relatives, friends, and strangers.

86

The Language of Covid-19

(April 21, 2020)

There's something in the language
that makes the old and familiar so novel.
It starts with a country's index case,
the carrier from whom the infection spreads.
Viral is no longer what social media celebrated
but a terrible affliction that is no laughing matter.
The tests come down to positive or negative
but who is fooled by positive that is negative
and negative that is positive in clinical parlance;
carriers showing symptoms or asymptomatic?

There's something in today's language
that makes the familiar usage suddenly archaic.
In every country where the terror flares, it peaks,
plateaus, and starts to curve; a drop that lowers
the blood pressure after threats of mass graves.
It has come to enrich tabulation and statistics
that leaders and health analysts put into models.

In one season the language wouldn't have experienced
a faster change of the familiar to the new—
frontline workers exposed because of no sufficient PPEs
and heroically form a significant percentage of fatalities.
It's the wish of the weak that it levels all humans and countries
but not too fast at that—Germany and South Korea come out
relatively unscathed; the colored among the rich bear the brunt.

Every language evolves as the people's experience
of what frightens and challenges their ingenuity
until they come out scarred but whole out of the woods.
There's surely something in today's language
that makes what we are used to and familiar new.

87

A Strange Disease Takes Over Kano

"A strange disease is killing quite a number," some said
when they noticed unusual activity at Kano* cemeteries.
Calling the name, they feared, would unleash its wrath
on bewildered folks. That was how the heavy toll had to
be explained until the scourge had slipped into and taken
over quarters, markets, and holy grounds in the historic city.
Currently published figures mock the extent of the random
devastation but it's real where burials are such a solemn duty.
Kano has been everyone's fear of Covic-19's ruthless rampage.

After several days of silence, a cry, not from the minaret,
to defang the monster responsible for infection and fatalities.
One cannot close one's ears and eyes to the havoc there
that is bound to spill out of secrecy into the public view
of neighbors and the media that first blew the whistle.
Covid-19 was a strange disease in its early appearance
in Wuhan and for some time silence and secrecy of burials
until local officials could not hold down the lid that blew out.
In Kano it's still a strange killing disease with a known name.

*Kano: a historic Muslim city of about eighteen million inhabitants and a trading
trans-Saharan hub in Northern Nigeria.

88

When Shall We Meet Again?

National borders were fading fast, thanks to globalization,
until the unannounced arrival of Covid-19 and its spread.
All of a sudden the proven deterrent and safety measure
called for closing of national borders to other nationals.
Nationality became the identification of folks who took
cosmopolitan, global, and world citizen as compliments.
The nation has become the haven to which you retreat
to live and battle to survive or die with fellow citizens
of governments that close their borders to foreign nationals.
The nationalists worldwide have for now won the struggle
for supremacy with maximum support of an invisible power.
What a movement out of course in the twenty-first century
that national borders separate people from each other into
Americans, Ethiopians, Italians, or Nigerians! My friend
whose identity is simply human, when shall we meet again?

89

As I See Things

(April 22, 2020)

There are the born gamblers
who exhibit the guts of brazen hunters
hoping to catch by hand the leopard alive
and be acclaimed instant heroes.
Many could be irrational because
of what they hope to win
even against all the odds out there.

There are others (like some of you or me)
who look down at what spot to put their feet;
too cautious to win big—they think of odds
against survival and take another route.
Seeing a leopard or what looks like it on their way
to riches, they either wait till the shadow
disappears or take another way however long.

The gamblers want to be rich in the face
of pestilence; their survival is another matter.
The others do not want to taunt
pestilence or fate to join the affluent;
they don't believe in a charmed life
though they even admire the gamblers' daredevilry
whose reasoning they consider suspect.

There are the born gamblers
who exhibit the guts of brazen hunters
hoping to catch by hand the leopard alive
and be acclaimed instant heroes.
But hard as it is, I'll prefer hunger
for several more weeks than
accept hazard pay in a time of Covid-19.

90

On Earth Day

(April 23, 2020)

Today's Earth Day.
Resulting from human preoccupation
with Covid-19, a 7/24 absorption,
the entire non-human population celebrate
their freedom; an exceptional season
when left alone to thrive on their own.
The orchestra of birds, insects, and animals
entertain themselves with abandon.

The lockdown should remain forever,
they wish those who give them no peace.
Why should others wish human folks evil,
curse them to be forever trapped in trepidation
of an invisible enemy on the loose
for them to live a better life?
Revolution is not only a human endeavor.
Others need it even more to bloom as now.

91

The Viral Resolve

You think it is over.
It is not; it rears its head
in another place. Expected or not,
so persistent, the stubbornness astonishes
in the war of attrition it wages.
When you are invisible
and the rest of the world trying
to hunt you down, you go viral;
more so as each nation has its strategy
sometimes at odds with many others
and you know that divided
the world would fall casualty
to the singular resolve of Covid-19
that also wants to live
as humans too want to.
This life or existence isn't only
a human property or preserve
but also for others, most of whom
non-human have suffered
at the hands of humans
who feel the world is theirs only
and not a shared planet
in which their law of survival
of the fittest could reign against them.
Who wants to die, human,
non-human, or virus?

92

This is Not the Time to Celebrate Age

(April 24, 2020)

It's not a time to celebrate age
when cast in a vulnerable category
a doctor can deny you a ventilator,
deny you life for a younger patient
as if at times some young ones don't
die before septuagenarians who live on.

This is not a time to celebrate age
and spill out wisdom from the mouth
for youths to take away and live with.
You're so dispensable and not treated;
you become a stigma for relatives
who are happy they have no oldies.

This is not a time to celebrate age
gracefully or not; age has become
a threat the world wants to dispose of.
In the grocery store, folks keep more
than distant so you don't infect them
because you are not only a scarecrow
but also a likely carrier of fatal viruses
nobody wants to catch and take home.

Instead of vacationing in paradise
that your huge account can take you to,
you stay sheltered in the basement
of the mansion you built a career to buy
and pray, if the doctors and nurses
pass you over to expire
without a ventilator in short supply
a million of which you can buy,
you might head into a refrigerated truck
for a dump pit in God-knows-where.
It's not the time to celebrate age.

93

Today's My Birthday

No day can be locked down from the calendar
and April 24 arrives with birthday expectations.
The past three years on this day I had been at
Myrtle Beach, Petersburg, and Havana with
the cheerful ambience of beaches in paradise
but here I am today at home under lockdown.

Today's my birthday.
I am carrying the haircut of two months ago;
no pedicure since salons are shut by order.
The gift certificates stare at me without hope
of early redemption—JC Penny and Burlington
owe me clothes that my family ordered for me.
No fancy restaurant on this day; no special cake.

Today's April 24 and must pass as every day
does but this year it passes without fanfare.
There's no gathering, no boxes or paper cards;
but the virtual party gladdens my heart—social
media outpourings of messages and memories
which translated to materials would clog me.

The spirit overwhelms me every minute
of the day so far and still in the morning.
The lighter everybody with gifts the more
passionate the Happy Birthday ringing
from those who love me and remember
on this day that cannot be locked down.
April 24 arrives with virtual celebrations.

94

The Same Questions without Answers

(April 25, 2020)

Another morning of the novel terror,
and the same questions:

when will one fly across the ocean to meet one's love?
When will schools reopen for face-to-face classes again?
Who will live in the pandemic state that is being
founded on the trail and litters of Covid-19?
When will all the shutters down lift up for light?

It has come to change the world from its familiar self,
but will there be change from the relentless uncertainty
into which it has plunged the world to be so shaken?
If the change becomes permanent, will this planet
be what has been or something different; a novel land?

It's too early for answers to the difficult questions
that paralyze the world into a helpless body;
too early for diviners to speak from their godhead.
It's not too late to know human limitations—not
every question can be answered; not every knot untied.

95

Bequeath Me Those Beautiful Virtues

Many are apportioning their property and income
according to proximity in affection and relationships;
attorneys sealing wills and leaving with secrets and smiles.

For the firefighter, give me your courage under heat;
for the doctor, your godhead in performing miracle cures;
for the old in ravaged homes, the wide lens of memory.

Don't leave only cash and companies to the living.
Leave your humility and stubbornness behind;
leave generosity that makes you happier the more you give.

All you out there in the pandemic writing or updating your will,
consider leaving behind your sense of sacrifice to the living;
consider giving reason and flexibility to your extremist kinsfolks.

I don't need anybody's cash or property because I will leave them
as they are leaving them. Bequeath me those beautiful virtues
that will make me and others more human than we have been.

96

We Knew It Would Come to This

(April 26, 2020)

We knew it would come to this:
it would be so easy once among us
for Covid-19 in its desperation
to recruit a large mercenary force
of politicians, traders, lords, hustlers,
and any whose heart beats on capital.

It amasses legions of fighters as it spreads
across the world; each country with more
than enough defenders of rights, capital,
and sacrificing others for their profits.
We knew it would come to this:
living or dying from the follies of others.

97

A Trickster's Tale

Covid-19 is fueling fake news
that distracts from eliminating it.
I think of the tortoise thrown
into hot water and saying it was
enjoying the punishment and only
cold water of rivers hurts or kills it.
Once the gullible ones released it
into a river, it swam away cackling
into freedom to do more mischief.
Fake news fuels Covid-19.

The coronavirus is harvesting fatalities
as fake news spreads miracle cures
that fuel the rage for more casualties
from among the quacks and bystanders.
The entire population deals with a trickster
able to confuse the heads of many who in
gossip make it seem an entertaining treat
for close contact after social distancing;
the proclaimed treatment fuels the rampage.
The gossip media fuels Covid-19.

98

When Tomorrow is Familiar

(April 27, 2020)

Some things are leaving and may never come back;
it's not in our power to hold them back. Others have come
and will never leave even if we want them to; it's not within
our power to drive away what came to visit and stay forever.

The strangeness of today may become familiar tomorrow
and we become permanent residents of a novel state.
We have to leave for good what has passed us into the past
and we are married to the stranger we have to live with.

If it were so simple, we would make things comfortable
but in a raging war we don't think beyond survival.
Where we now go is different from where we came from
that has forever lost the ability to keep us in that long ago.

If we are at the end of one world, at the beginning of what
nobody knows, we don't know how it will treat us.
Nobody knows tomorrow makes sense in the pandemic
taking us elsewhere we can't predict will be hospitable.

99

When Each Day Dawns

Every moment like every day creates its
own answer to the riddle, limited because
there's no solution; no unknotting of the mystery
beyond the trying to solve and overcome
the handicap fate has set to keep one guessing.

A voice from deep in the past fills up the day's
void and that's as far as you can come out—
often levitate from the doldrums believing that
however terrible some beauty will launch through;
such moments rescue from what you can't control.

This day dawns with sunlight breaking through
the net of gloom that news casts to stifle us at home;
there's life and laughter that save from the infection
and the day's tallies that mock every effort
to think of doom as a trap set deliberately to kill.

This morning memories of youth flood me—
as a fisherman setting hooks and often surprised
by the catch—huge mudfish I could barely lift;
tapping rubber and driven home by a storm
from nowhere after a cool and calm beginning.

We are finding what we didn't set out to seek,
discovering new ways to laugh out of pain
and live on farther away from the starting point.
And that's life: it could be so sweet and bitter
as it enriches one day to survive days ahead.

100

Preparing for Surprises

(April 28, 2020)

I tell the strong they can't be prepared for every surprise.

A virus slips into and terrorizes a superpower battleship in the Pacific
and there's SOS to those on land and in the air; these too crying for help.
What a shame for an invisible enemy to neutralize the mighty ship
that the best builders handed to be armed to the teeth for the best sailors!
Commanding captain and fighters jump into water despite the ethics,
ready to defy odds and survive sharks and pirates than coronavirus;
they lost the lessons of courage from the naval academy they attended
since big guns, bombs, and missiles in the hold cannot defend them.

Covid-19 assaults the fearsome battleship and finds it so easy
to neutralize and disable a superpower vessel dominating the Pacific.
There's no superpower in the face of the novel virus invisible to all;
only humans for life's sake fleeing for safety in distant self-isolation.
I hear of the shameful capitulation of the great battleship in the Pacific
and realize how the small have smitten big ones. We see for ourselves
those preparing for war for a whole century still caught unprepared
for this war against a virus that makes expensive weapons useless toys.

I tell the strong they can't be prepared for every surprise.

101

Futuristic World

Broken keys of the piano wailing through streets
drums without parchments messaging through eons
the world a vast tent leaking acid rain from many points
from the tears of powerful nationals of a poor state
Olympic medaled sprinters taunting spirits clubfooted
the world inhabited by a species of flat-backed tortoises
that fly carrying passengers from pain to a celestial haven.

The reviled ethics of antediluvian society returns
with human sacrifice sanitized with prayers in hospitals
birth no more a physical exercise but droplets from the nose
everybody walking backwards not to collide with imps
with eyes twinkling red and pointing to perils ahead.
After Covid-19's arrival there's nothing the world
can't become; nothing not imagined as change—

life's a wailing broken keyboard of a piano in the street
drums without parchment messaging through eons.

102

This Coronavirus Sef

(April 29, 2020)

My people, this coronavirus sef not im be the evil spirit
pastors and congregation dem dey curse every Sunday

not im deprive us of better health
not im dey kill people dear to us

no be im panel-beat lungs of people
wen never smoke for dem life

no be im send malaria go kill so many
no be im bring stroke and complications?

This Covid-19 don so tey e be with us
in different shapes wen im dey work for devil.

No be im make rich and poor dey fear die
no be im make proud person dey cool down

no be im dey attack our people wen dey die after brief
illness, make dem dey die wen life dey sweet them

no be im dey with us as friend, family, neighbor
but na witch wen dey kill us for coven and celebrate?

E don so tey Covid-19 dey among us o.
We no know na im dey do havoc we dey suffer.

Na im you dey look for and e dey there with you.
Who no know go know say e don so tey e dey with us.

You don one day hear tortoise dey mess?
No be im smell wen dey kill we know?

103

Final Solution

Na all we dey do na im Covid-19 dey use against us.
Who get opportunity and e no go use am?
If person don old and im get diabetes, hypertension,
or any of those conditions wen dey kill people,
Corona go strike the person. No be point of least
resistance soldiers dey follow for war? No be win
we dey fight for? Corona don learn all im tricks from us.

Not be diseases we know Covid-19 dey use against us?
Person go think say na fever or cough na im get;
e go think say na stroke or na blood clot im get
but gbaam! Corona don bring down the person.
Na im bring malaria, stroke, cough, or wetin call?
Na im bring sickness come the world you dey blame am?
E dey use wetin e get to fight the way e fit fight.

Diseases dey borku before now and e dey use available
resources to fight e own war against this patch-patch world
wen get too many problems. Some be too rich where
plenty people poor; some people feel dey better pass
others and many dey boast say na dem get power;
some don advance too close to God and others
still stuck where they start a thousand years ago.
Make Covid-19 resolve problems for the world.

As people selfish na so e selfish;
as capitalism no dey make people considerate
na so e be for Covid-19 work—ruthless, e no dey
look back whether people dey suffer or die no concern am.
Na our human weapons na im Covid-19 dey use against us.

104

Coping With Covid-19

(April 30, 2020)

I have already done six weeks of hiding
from catching a virus nobody knows
for sure where it is and where it isn't.

Today I redoubled my usual one-hour walk
by taking turns I had never taken
and perhaps won't take again.
I dress for no reason; nowhere to go really
since I'll stay at home as I do nowadays.
We will talk of face covers, which I refuse
to call masks that I leave for ancestors
come back to warn us with entertainment.
The numbers on television still unsettle the mind.

Before I realize it, the day's far gone preparing
for tomorrow when my mind and body will device
novel ways to cope with Covid-19 and the lockdown.

105

Intermissions

(May 1, 2020)

It's the intermissions
we pray to last.

Not the main event that goes
on forever with a thousand episodes
breathless times that consume us.

Yes, it's the intermissions
during which we exhale
and even when wordless
we convey love to another
that we were too preoccupied
to notice in the mad pursuit
of worldly trends.

It's the intermissions
in which we have little time to exhale
but convey love
that we wish to last.

106

Wielding the Shield of the Gods

For those fortunate to catch
the mild form of the coronavirus
whose recovery rate is almost a hundred percent,
taking warm water is a proven cure
as well as chloroquine, a cocktail of ginger,
lemon, and garlic, or engaging steam treatment.
Take pepper soup and you're cured of Covid-19!
Take the Madagascar syrup and you are up in days!
Those the gods have shielded from death
contract fever or cough that goes on its own.
As for the less than two percent marked
by destiny to be casualties, they die at the hands
of expert doctors of otherwise miracle cures.
Such is life that planting in the year of blessings
turns one to become a prosperous farmer, but plant
the best crops in the wrong season and you lose all!
That's why there are many cures for a terrible
affliction from which most escape its fatality.

107

Tomorrow Will Become Today

Tomorrow is coming and many are hurrying
to overtake it or arrive long before others—
they want to experience morning dew and have
a huge bargain from the merchants of dawn.

They are hurrying to beat dawn at its game
of early arrival by setting out before a wink
of light as if to beat tomorrow in a race
to arrive before it's a new day.

Many are hurrying to open the market
before what infested it to be closed
has been disinfected; the crowds still
a danger yet many want to march through.

The day will dawn, tomorrow will become *today*
and the market will open. Why the stampede to
where you'll have more than enough time to spend;
why hasten before dawn to beat dawn for early arrival?

Beware of overstepping what cripples
by hurrying to where you'll spend
the rest of your life in one routine!
Beware of precipitate lifting of lockdown!

108

The Past Has Come to Cheer Me Up

(May 2, 2020)

The past has come to cheer me up—
the camaraderie in Warri streets lost to civil-war days
and the historic love of boisterous youth in Yerwa*;

they come to cheer me up from gloom
that Covid-19 casts over the entire earth;
the past has come to lead me out of it.

Despite social distancing and self-isolation
that keep me out of sight for these seven weeks,
today another dawn hits me with special illumination;

they have come to lift me—
lockdown and self-isolation have thrust me
out there into the hearts of long ago.

They have come to light up the present
with glowing images that go so far
there's faith in never losing what we love;

they have come to me through surprise
text messages and phone calls across eons
in pre-dawn hours making waking a delight;

they have come to wake me to another day.
I can see the lockdown lifting; the first steps out.
The past has surely come to cheer me up.

*Yerwa: old name for Maiduguri, Borno State.

109

You Narrowly Missed the Casualty List

(for Boris Johnson and Chris Cuomo)

By the time you fall into a delirium
talking to deceased parents calling your pet name
as if they were visiting in your sitting room
their eyes blinking red and green in the dim-lit room
and when they rise to leave forbid you
from getting up to escort them out into the dark,

know you have reached a formidable fork
where taking either right or left means
a doomed path to the land of no-return
but lightning at the crucial moment of choice
wakes you and you realize you are still
in the same hospital bed in a Covid-19 ward
and you have not slipped from the hands of
doctors and nurses struggling to keep you alive.

110

Seasons of Migration

(May 3, 2020)

There are seasons for migration.

In one season of migration
those who dared desert and waves to leave
arrived where they transformed into
groomed figures in their new homes—
the ugly toned into glowing beauties,
those who escaped penury in their lives
found wealth in dollar accounts;
and those who would have rotted
thrived to become stars in a new world.

But Covid-19 arrives to test migration.
When Italy, Spain, and America roll out bodies,
the fortunate immigrants ask themselves
if it's worth facing death outside one's homeland,
if it's worth it living through a plagued season
after celebrating life for decades of success,
worth it not having one's grave however modest
to mark transition in one's birthplace
rather than be thrown into a foreign dump pit.

There are different seasons for migration.

111

The Politics of Covid-19

(May 4, 2020)

Surely, the politics of Covid-19 is glocal—
it feeds Trump's theme of Jinping cheating on him.
But it's the local that catches my fancy—
those who see the ogre ravaging their land as not there
in Kano or Washington; living outside the real world, and
acknowledging when further denial exposes them as fools.
They incite protesters to lift the lockdown, and only
a second wave will prove them nincompoops of science.
Many play with figures; honesty a scarce commodity—
they lie so shamelessly you feel like spitting at their faces
since the lies pouring out of their mouths, really poison,
amplify fatalities and despair in the land they fight to rule.
Politics drives everything; matters of life and death—its
practitioners won't care as long as it consolidates their power
and accounts in risking other people's lives; nothing else.
Pity we can't eschew politics from the war against Covid-19!

112

The Ordinance

(May 5, 2020)

With supernatural power to randomly infect
in its invisibility, Covid-19 goes round, a spirit,
to implement its hidden program. It seeks hard
to seal faces it catches with divine ordinance.
How else explain survival or fatality of those
picked from millions that have to live or die?

Those it infects appear to have been brought its way
from out-of-reach positions to assailable points.
And I think of those who shouldn't have traveled
but did, those offered enviable positions that exposed
them to what would doom them to the plague's toll.
It has to be destiny for the hawk to swoop down
to snatch away one chick from among a large brood.

Covid-19 goes round, a spirit, to stamp the seal
of divine ordinance on faces it attempts to kill.

113

Surprised Not Surprised

(May 6, 2020)

I would have been surprised if no heroes came out
of the existential war against the novel breed of monsters;
I would have been surprised if no carriers emerged
to cleanse the land with their blood to save the world,
and they turned out many in and outside of hospitals;
they were there among those locked in bunkers at home
but from isolation contributed more than a simple share.

I would have been surprised at no heroes coming out
but surprised at the high number of fifth columnists
pressuring the human chain for Covid-19 to break in;
I am surprised at the astounding number of profiteers
trafficking on fear, desperation, helplessness, and even
deaths for the windfall of a lifetime without conscience;
they stink in their voracious corruption of the human spirit.

I would have been so surprised if no villains showed up
but surprised at the record number and passion of those
stepping out to be carriers to free the world of the plague;
I would have been surprised if Covid-19 despite its villainy
did not mobilize that number of fifth columnists from among us—
the season of the coronavirus has made it so conducive
for the division of humans into heroes and villains!

114

Today the Sun Rises

Today the sun rises.
I was faithless to be depressed at nightfall.
Today the sun rises
and in these spring days of nature's bloom
it was faithless to take night as sudden winter.
Today the sun rises
and light's warmth and the rich tapestry
of flora and fauna, the supreme art of life
all bring out testaments of divine gifts.
Covid-19 brings gloom and doom
but today the sun rises
for all of us—humans and non-humans.
I look up and see glowing sunlight;
I look around and beauty surrounds me.
I was faithless to have gone to bed depressed
by the terrible toll reeling across the screen.
Today the sun rises
and I regain my faith.

115

Double Challenge

(May 7, 2020)

It dawns for me in two countries, two time zones.
I can only live in one at a time. I suffer the handicap
of property ownership; however many homes and
citizenships, only one serves its purpose at a time.
Who's twice endowed can also be doubly challenged.

It dawns for me in two countries at a time—
the tropical always precedes the temperate; the sun
travels westward as I also chose to travel once
but now regularly make it both ways; away and home.
I am two minds, two hearts but one person for whom
the sun rises twice. A polygamist, I can't love equally;
so much one heart can love, one head can keep as memory.

In times of a pandemic, twice worried by horrible news
of both countries, two continents, two time zones—
I even suffer headaches for the two and take Panadol for both.
One fears for both countries, prays for two loves
and looks forward to this unique love to thrive
after life returns to as normal as changed times can be.
Who's twice endowed can also be doubly challenged.

116

Flow

(May 8, 2020)

I went with the flow before Covid-19.
I trusted all would be right in whatever I did.
Once Covid-19 the incarnate trickster arrived,
the flow constricted my amplitude and got irregular.
Only time remains regular, the unperturbed lord
exercising suzerainty over all humans and viruses.

There's another flow the coronavirus cannot disrupt—
it cannot hold back the hands of the clock;
it cannot stop the approaching summer.
It can attack humans but most don't succumb to it,
and that's a major limitation for who chose to be invisible
in sowing fire seeds of death wherever people live on earth.

I still follow the flow though Covid-19 attempts
to totally disrupt it to no avail. I am scared
but still sleep, rise, and do my daily chores.
It may be strong but not invincible; we both obey
the flow time imposes on us as the destiny we share.
All will be well after the trickster's inevitable defeat.

117

Partial Lifting of Lockdown

(May 9, 2020)

We look for hope to clutch to.
And so while there's no letup of life threats,
not to talk of a curve somewhere to hang on to,
figures still climbing the mountain and not peaked,
many pour out once a partial lifting of lockdown's
announced as a sign that things are good and stampede
out of the prison houses of our homes; ants in sunshine.
The subjective triumphs over the objective for desperadoes,
and so we latch to hope as if the terrible season is over
when the doom has not lifted. We have become so
fearful of the present and the future that we go backwards
to clutch to hope and live more dangerously outdoors.
We choose self-divination when the seer's message is bleak
and celebrate self-liberation from shame of hiding from a virus
by pouring out like soldier ants into the sun that will sting them
in the adventure they so much enjoy but exposes them to dying.
We clutch to hope in the face of no letup in life threats.

118

It Takes More Than One

It takes more than one to be well
as it takes more than the other to be sick.
There's always the possibility of infection
and this manifests in more ways than one
in others sharing the same planet and humanity.
The infected and those fearing infection are sick;
only the good health of all is everybody's wellbeing.
Isn't that why our elders say we are our kinsfolks' keepers
and they in return shield themselves to protect us?

119

Carriers

(May 10, 2020)

They aren't defenders at all but Wall Street fodder;
doctors, nurses, meat packers, grocery and department
store cashiers and others in the frontline—school and city
bus drivers, housekeepers, and construction workers—
least prepared to defend the land they serve with their body.
They have direct contact with fellow human beings who
need them for the basics of life though they are paid only
a pittance to serve as Wall Street fodder for the corporate class.

For all their exposure to defend those who use them, they
remain at the very bottom of the scale in wealth distribution
and as the first to suffer most from infection or lockdown,
they are easily lured with hazard pay to be back to face peril.
They are involuntary carriers in the fight against pestilence.

Of course, there are those making fortune from Wall Street,
who in their secure boardrooms give orders to frontliners;
they drive workers impoverished by their greed to slave on
to keep the capitalist cog oiled and running smoothly for profit.
The workers want to be self-reliant but can't be in the system.
It's a pity those in the frontline are least prepared to hold back
the invisible virus they are fighting from despoiling the land
because they aren't defenders at all but only Wall Street fodder.

120

Who We Are

The coronavirus brings out who and what we are.
A pastor curses the president for ordering shutdown of churches,
the platform for offerings and collections for a lavish lifestyle;
the anti-Christ has arrived and Covid-19 is only a weapon.

A sectional leader argues about fighting back southern groups
deploying a virus to depopulate and emasculate northerners—
the ethnic cleansing they had feared in the federation has begun;
they won't hold back but come out to fight malicious rivals; viruses.

Covid-19 remains a mystery when it appears and it's not
the one causing infections and fatalities but rivals and enemies;
it's only humans who don't wish people of advantage well
and smite those they relish their fortune with mysterious deaths.

Of course, you can't blame a virus for what's happening to folks;
it can't be jealous, wicked, or seeking economic or political advantage—
it must be human carriers of trouble attempting to hurt others.
The coronavirus brings out glaringly who and what we are!

121

Zigzagging Graph

(May 11, 2020)

Fear waxes and wanes and its graph zigzags
up and down depending on what informed voice
you hear, morning or evening, and your unstable mood.

The President, cheered by a task force, talks of an expedited vaccine
and hope rises to the point of euphoria to dissipate fear—
soon the stranded frequent flyer will take to the skies; free and fine.

But in a sober briefing the governor knocks down the scaffolds
for launching a vaccine and warns of individual responsibility
to save others and ourselves from unspeakable fatalities.

And by the time health experts talk tentatively that the virus will go
but will take time, perhaps two years if we are fortunate to vaccinate
all and find a treatment for all the infected with an established protocol,
I am beyond panic attack by the scare of hope taking too long to save us.

And all these beside the graphic images of hospitals wheeling out
cadavers through backdoors while protests in the street to open up
as if telling folks the virus will be around with us for quite a while
isn't opening up enough about mortal ferocity than reckless freedom.

There's confusing graph movement; south and north, and backwards.
And so as hope brings vaccines and treatments to celebrate,
fear waxes and wanes as its graph zigzags up and down.

122

Hubris

To die of a shark attack during a beach picnic
and not on land after violating self-isolation

to carry placards to lift the lockdown against the plague
and testing positive after contact with fellow protesters

to say there's no novel virus but only a millennial hoax
and within weeks end up in the ICU with its symptoms

to have more than enough to purchase hundreds of ventilators
whose shortage makes doctors pass you by for younger patients

to be so confident of self-defense with an armory at home
and not seeing the virus to fire at when it breaks in to infect

to hate crowds and noise and wishing for a quiet life
and in a quarantine lonely and praying for companionship

it's the call of the coronavirus that many have to respond to;
what the Greeks have been passing for centuries to every age.

123

It Matters Not Where I Would Have Been

(May 12, 2020)

There are things we will never know
because the pandemic makes them unknowable;
the many wistful *ifs*, if what happened didn't
but *would haves* if nothing happened to plans ahead.

It matters not where I would have been at this time
without the shutdown everywhere to fight the threat;
I, who would have been a continent across the Atlantic,
scheduled to have arrived at Abuja today but didn't.

What message would I have sent here from my natal home;
what images of rain there would drown summer sunshine?
What am I doing now that wouldn't have been done, if away;
and what would have inspired me to sing a different song?

What migratory birds would stop over at River Park Estate*?
What would I see retracing streams of my birthplace to their sources,
and what summer I missed left to guesses of advantages of two
worlds? There today doesn't matter because I am not there.

For long free, I jumped into planes to relish flight and freedom
but now bound to my *away* home a vulnerable one needing care;
there are things we will never know if they happened or didn't.
Today I walk in my arboreal neighborhood of the ghost town.

*River Park Estate: a residential area on Airport Road, Abuja.

124

Relatives

Relatives I didn't know I had lived unknown
to me in the same town, country, and world.
We are deep planning to survive the pandemic
in isolation from others, including all relatives.

I never knew I had affluent relatives before; now they
would rather save their bodies like me than keep wealth.
I didn't know my brothers, sisters, and cousins of other races
until my blood plasma matched theirs for treatment and cure.

I didn't know I had so many relatives, indeed the entire
human population, until the novel virus opened my already
opened but not seeing eyes to the genes of fear, helplessness,
and hope we share. I didn't know everybody was my relative.

125

When Life Was Too Sweet

(May 13, 2020)

We reached a stage in life so sweet and convenient—
one summoned whatever one wanted to be delivered
at the doorstep or ordered to take away a dish one likes.
We exercised a godhead that made our heads swell and
careless; we thought of nothing beyond human capabilities,
migrating to Mars or the Moon or at least take a vacation
and the coronavirus leaped out of Wuhan to challenge us.
This was a novel bone too big for the global dog to bite.

For most, struggling to stay safe consumed them
and thoughts of big things shut down for how
to purchase toilet paper and face covers. Shrunk,
humans are cutting down their future expectations.
With infestations forbidding from excesses, there's
an invisible one to suppress fantasies, control freedom
to state borders or even restrict movement within
nations—the breaking of borders as a hobby arrested.
Struggling to survive, a vaccine or cure consumes the future.

The favorite child has suddenly lost the favorite status.
At the moment one doesn't have to do anything; life stops
when movement is no longer taken for granted with global
favors and migration. A virus shut the world down
to take things easy, struggle with mortality for some time
and not assume gods of humans; struggle to be alive,
take steps backward, go back in years, and then exhale
to restart. That's life; the change after being too sweet.
It is the novel bone too big for the global dog to bite.

126

I Embrace the Inevitable

Today I embrace the inevitable.
I woke and turned on the television
I had blacked out for days as I did
my social media platforms. There was
too much of death to trip anyone off,
with the experts forewarning of doom
that brought me to the verge of insomnia.

Today I thrust my chest forward; no fleeing.
These few days I reflected: a storm abates;
even the civil war I witnessed abated and
despite casualties, "no victor, no vanquished."

Now I get back to the screen where
at the last time Covid-19 raged fiercely.
Behold, it has not abated with figures fueled
by controversies of capitalists and politicians
with legions of global utilitarian protesters.
I won't switch off but watch the toll mounting
to the peak of the Everest. I see other casualties
in two-mile long queues for food for the hungry.

I won't turn away from the disquieting
images of pestilence that's the daily reality.
I can't live in another world of denial or fear;
I'll sit and watch the terrible reality we live in.
Today I embrace the inevitable
and not run from the life inflicted on us.

127

The Questioner

Day breaks and I sit in a chair.
After eating I am back to the same chair.
I keep busy and alive sitting in that chair.

Does the chair know what's in my mind?
Does it shiver with me when figures roll out?
Does the chair know how far my thoughts travel?

It is the season for the vulnerable to be cautious
and so I stay at home to be safe for tomorrow.
I stay at home to avoid falling into disaster.

Does the house love me for living in it?
Does it even know I am using it for protection?
If I owe the house, how does it get my gratitude?

At night sleep lifts me to another planet.
It takes me through experiences I'd rather leave
to avoid hurts to my mind and heart.

Does night regale in distracting me from the pandemic?
Does night's dream and daylight's fear cancel themselves?
Does it set me up for the day's resistance I need?

I sit in my chair at home to pass the day
for night to fulfill the destiny of dawn.
I am the questioner living on the unanswerable.

128

Love in the Time of the Coronavirus

There was love in the time of cholera.
Now there's love but perils litter pathways
to trysts—there are no ports at both ends
to receive us; no harbors for ships to dock.
We can't enter the other's land from where we're
stuck, can't freight feelings for delivery to the other.
There's love we can't control, and that's the virus's
scheme to test tenacity of hearts and of course destiny
till it opens the air and ports to meet at some date
and tell stories in songs of triumphs over perils.
There's deep love in the time of the coronavirus.

129

Love is a War

As you know, it's the coronavirus.
It has kept us apart to the point
of breaking human resolve. It allows
us to use FaceTime and video calls
because it overlooks global products
of advancement for human access.
We see and talk every day but that's not it.
It is not forbidding love but threatening
overflying the world with repercussions.
It's a tyrant denying us consummation
and our desires for all the flames they stoke
keep raging. We cannot yet be together.
As you know, it's the coronavirus
that tries to break the resolve of lovers.
But fighters, we resolve to overcome.

130

Trees

It's the trees that have nowhere to go,
habitats of squirrels, birds, and other beings,
that catch my attention this morning.

They stand in spring's splendor, coiffured green,
good-looking, flushed, and healthy as they can be.
They are in love with rainfall and sunshine
and I don't know which they love more for life's sake.

It's the trees, roots, trunks, branches, and leaves
that fill me with pageantry and tenacity of being.
Sometimes they face the serious challenge of storms
when they conjure strength from deep down the earth.

Who will not be happy to be serenaded by birds
of colorful plumes and honeyed voices? Who will
not be buoyed up by the liveliness of other lives?
They go out and return to smack you with memories.

By nature, they need no social distancing to be safe;
they won't ever self-isolate because they stand
upright where the soil nourishes them, rain or sun.

It's the plants that have nowhere to go
that catch my attention this morning.
I learn from non-humans to feel good.

131

Months of Our Lives

These several months of our lives
do not only arrest forward movement
but threaten daily with mortal fury.
We stay indoors far from others, and
practice hygiene lessons all over again.

We'll celebrate overcoming the coronavirus
in a parade of victors after a terrible war
in which our losses—time and possessions—
count for nothing as long as we survive
the pandemic months of our lives.

132

Staying Safe for the Day

(May 14, 2020)

To where and for what do I take my day to be safe?

The early morning walk is a debt I owe to my body and so
will cover the sidewalks of the Birnam Wood* neighborhood
to maintain relationship with trees, birds, and other nonhumans.
I'll stay at home now clinical to wash hands with or without dirt.

Without moving from home to keep in touch with relatives
and friends who remember and care for me than I ever thought
and are taking care of themselves as I am, I'll travel to multiple
states and countries. You can't believe that by day's end, I would
have crossed a dozen borders without passport to chat and be current.

I must listen spellbound to the bird that dutifully sings to me
wistfully from a nest in my birthplace. When that's happening
I wouldn't know time passes, and that song heals all my maladies.
It won't be a day without sitting in the chair that has become
a ritual site for me to read, write, and recite chants to Aridon**
who won't leave me alone as I also won't quit my benefactor.

And so I will take today to where and what I want us to be
and not complain about a virus. That's what it is to be safe for me.

*Birnam Wood: a residential area of Charlotte, North Carolina.
**Aridon: Urhobo god of memory and muse of the poet

133

I, of Another Age

(May 15, 2020)

I, the hypochondriac already sick with dreaded symptoms
before Covid-19 strikes me, must be driving other folks nuts.
I must be too timid and unbalanced that I fear my shadow;
they are the brave who must liberate the land from my type;
they must liberate markets and places from their lockdown.

The others can't allow my kind afraid to exercise the freedom
the Constitution enshrines to prevail and leave them bound.
To them I belong far back to the Stone Age without liberty;
I belong to the prehistoric time of fear filled with headhunters
and one could not move freely or live as a real human being.

I am one of those bringing down the Stock Market from its peak
with needless panic of confronting or contracting an invisible thing.
They would rather have hypochondriacs dead and leave them enjoy,
have opponents of the Constitution out if they wouldn't enjoy rights
than live and set them back to a bygone age they don't want back.

What a fool not to drive to the tavern for a pint of ale to be spritely;
what a drag not to go to the mall to fill trolleys and swipe your cards,
or not go to the beach in America and soak in summer's sea water!
To them the toll must be a conspiracy to scare them out of paradise.
I must be driving them nuts and setting them back to a bygone age.

134

Living Light

(May 16, 2020)

After decades of acquiring possessions and property,
carrying the ponderous loads all along and pressured,
life all of a sudden, thanks to the coronavirus, is light.

The virus has simplified human desires to the minimum,
even taunts greed if it can bear so much in a raging war.
Much we can do without: new clothes, gadgets, and toys.

The struggle to escape infection and death makes one
to drop possessions that slow and incapacitate one to fall,
preferring to be light; everything else an encumbrance.

One wakes, eats, and does not make shopping a priority,
keeps distant from others and obeys novel regulations,
and sits at home and hops out for the needed to stay safe.

No trolley loads, no contracts for new homes or property.
When there's life and what can protect it, all's bearable.
Life all of a sudden, thanks to the coronavirus, is so light.

135

A Time of Stories

More than at any time this is the time of stories.
Everybody has a story to tell.
I have a story for you, and so listen!
I listen to other people's stories as they hear mine.

The ear couldn't be more receptive
to cacophonies of old music turn to melodies;
every sound affirms life and heals from maladies.

In the pandemic season we are different but the same
and we couldn't be more the same humans than before.
The stories are ongoing and more will come our way.

I have heard stories that bring cold, fevers, and tremors;
heard stories of escapes at both ends and of casualties.
There are untold stories since who should tell them left
with heart-wrenching tales and can't return to tell them.

Still among us stories that will never be heard;
as in life, not everything goes according to plan—
not every mouth can tell what's in the head or heart.

More than at any time this is the time of stories.
There are stories to tell one like no other heard
and yet part of everybody's life and more unheard.
We pick ourselves together and that's one story too.

136

Change

(May 17, 2020)

They say everybody likes change.
We have had change in yearly car models
and spring fashion shows for summer trends—
we miss Milan, Paris, and New York for handbags,
aphrodisiac perfumes, and new fabric cuts.

But not every change is welcome.

In the Covid-19 pandemic season of 2020
many folks resist the new fashion trends of face
covers, social distancing, and clinical behaviors;
hence the protests for life to return to normal.
What can be normal when normalcy changes
and a new normal out of today's strangeness?

Not every normal is a choice thing.

We couldn't be more confused about new
and old than now; whatever's new turns old;
more so when there's no choice in the matter—
the imposition on the helpless and clueless;
those who choose and now selected for
a challenge experiment to save everybody.
Survival needs disrupt habits and set trends.

The world is capable of turning upside down.

137

So Far

(May 18, 2020)

We don't know how far
we have gone
until challenged on the way
and we realize
the much far we have gone
ahead of where we should be
and then have to stand still
or fall back
before a forward thrust
into the unknown
we think we know
but unprepared
for uncertainties
of going too fast
to a place
even millennia will not take us
because there's no limit
to a journey without end.
The coronavirus has its place
in the scheme of things
in where we are today
and it may not be in control
of tomorrow not to talk
of the tomorrows ahead
and on and on.

138

No Queries

Nobody queries what I use my time for anymore.
My friend abroad consumes most of the hours as if
leaving me off means more leisure with my partner
who chooses to ignore my constant daily video calls.
The two women could be of different minds but have
a deal to help me through a hard period stuck indoors.
No-one wants to make the difficult decision of starting
trouble when there's enough trouble already keeping safe.

139

To the Hand

(May 19, 2020)

In your zest, you overreach yourself
to be stigmatized as a carrier dispensing
dirt to the body—infect only the hand
and you have infected the entire body!
Yet none wants to be handless; helpless
with much to handle, touch, and carry.

You have so much service to perform
but hold back from picking the nose;
keep from eyes and mouth lest what
sticks to you gets ingested into the body.

O hand that carries viruses but also cleans,
you have thrust yourself at the center
of a pandemic; prime infection suspect!
But you are also the one looked up to
to save the body and the community
by only one act: wash, wash, and wash!

140

Touch

Once hands clasped
to show how inseparable we are.
There were elaborate rites of greeting—
cheek to cheek; Hollywood love
incomplete without kissing.
Now elbow touch is in vogue
and friends and relatives don't
go that far as to punch with fists.
We huddled in spaces for warmth,
sat or stood to cheer or play games.
Today love comes after safety concerns;
wellness a priority to keep distant for.
A new world culture is born.

141

Something Else

In everything
there's something else
and in that something else
something and something else
until there's something unrelated
but related
and other things.

Coronavirus is such a thing.
It's something, a novel coronavirus
that's something else
and on and on
until it's an enemy
with friendly offshoots
and no longer a virus
but something else
meant to challenge life
as we knew it.

142

Everything is Connected

I am getting up late by my own standard;
still early for others on a late May morning
at 6:15 during a lockdown under protest.
I didn't look at the time before I slept
after watching for over two hours
far beyond my normal bedtime of 11
a documentary on Mobutu Sese Seko
relived the pain of Africa's tragic fortune
set up abroad by Belgium and America
that created a monster to devour the continent's
creative aspirations by eliminating Lumumba
and worse still installing a fool king of their like.
You may wonder what this has to do with coronavirus.
To me everything is connected since others predict
Africans are least prepared for a proclaimed danger.
I got up late this morning though too early for others
whose long hand I see in the tardiness elsewhere.

143

Where We Differ

I hear in Italy, Sweden, and elsewhere
they pass over the old—sixty-five and over—
to conserve life-saving equipment and medications
for the young; they leave homes to their vulnerable fate.

We have no homes for the old to be out of family care.
Rather, every elder lives with children and adults
in an unbreakable bond of the unborn, living, and ancestors.
Our Mother Hens will put their lives in harm's way
to cover their broods. Every son defends mother and
father against whatever threatens their lives and wellbeing.

The young can only grow fully among their elders
who they will keep alive for their own total health.
They are the libraries of knowledge in proverbs.
Every life should matter as each has a place in
communities where humans live under Covid-19.

144

Dance of Defiance

(May 20, 2020)

Among my not-well-known people
they dance in defiance of death
which they don't want to cow them;
they so much love to enjoy life to the full
despite death lurking and poaching a number,
at burials they sing, dance, and drown in liquor.

Today, there are groups of people
who subscribe to the dance of defiance.
They defy the coronavirus, the carrier of maladies
and death, by damning precautions to stop its spread.
They defy in protests, workplaces, congregating without
limit, and swearing not to wear face covers to taunt the killer.

There's so much of the old in the new
and the new in the old in human behavior
when folks don't acknowledge things have changed.

145

It's the Coronavirus

(May 21, 2020)

My ninety-two-year old mom is bedridden thousands of miles away
and her first son, family priest, cannot fly to touch and cheer her up.
It's the coronavirus whose spread shut down nations and airspaces.

One's heartwarming friend lives an ocean apart and her minstrel
and magician, healer of maladies, can't transform to meet her
to sing or touch her to be happy because of the strict lockdown.

My daily gym visits to do something stopped three months ago
and because gyms will be last to reopen in the tentative schedule,
I am left helpless with serious health concerns, and no virus cares.

The profession I committed my life is challenged with closures
because face-to-face contact is forbidden to arrest viral infection,
and I lose passion for classroom theatrics to sedate online teaching.

It's the coronavirus setting me up as vulnerable and making me
not carry out my natural responsibilities to myself and others.
I am out of joint with myself, living without what gives me zest.

146

Newly Discovered Beauty

Suddenly their beauty entrances me
as if I have not seen them this way
in the same wooded neighborhood
we have shared for twenty-six years.

The late spring pines, maples, junipers,
and others flaunt beauty and splendor at me—
they stand at attention for me to admire
their erect and coiffured bodies one after another;
the rich texture of barks, sleek limbs, and fine tone.
The squirrels race across road and grass to climb
tree trunks and branches purring majestically.
More than before I watch birds in compelling
beauty of plumes and luster singing—I listen
to the philharmonic tunes of the avian orchestra.
All these as the rising sun and Carolina blue sky
cheer me up to enthrall myself in beauties around.

They all awaken me to the new day
and in the communion something ties us together
human and non-human beings in dialogue relishing
reciprocal respect and being cherished for what we are.
They possess me with newly discovered beauty.

147

The Challenge

During my walk, I see myself climbing a hill
on a cool wet morning and I suddenly breaking a sweat.
A spirit seems to be pushing me back as I struggle forward.
I realize I am at a stage where the trial slows me down
before where will accelerate me downhill without effort
to regain balance and confidence as a tireless walker.
And I think of the world at a standstill or fighting regression
until the pandemic abates and we reach the right point
when a creative impulse will explode to propel us
farther than we would have gone without the challenge.

148

An Implacable Shield

May 22, 2020)

My wife posts JESUS on all doors in our house.
Born Catholic, her day without Mass is incomplete.
I practice poetry and reason for which I am glad.
At ordinary times I would have torn down the postings
and told her to strictly follow protocol to avoid infection.
To her, my herbal mixture to repel feverish maladies is juju.

I believe she believes she's conscripted JESUS as a guard
and because invisible like the virus will shield us from peril.
In these days when power reinforces power and we need
an implacable shield against an invisible enemy, who am I
not to deploy her faith and every possible tool to win the war?
My wife has posted JESUS on every door in the house.

149

After Insane Budgets

(May 23, 2020)

Keeping safe from what one cannot see
is a different challenge from what's visible;
keeping away from what's so evasive it penetrates
pores to destroy every vital organ is guesswork.
It's not seen coming from somewhere until it strikes.

The thief blows no whistle; it has no weight for noise
that will forewarn of an intruder before it arrives.
Coronavirus is a global witch and so supernatural
it disperses ailments and death in its noiseless trail.
Worse, it has no heart or conscience for compassion.

How on earth do you keep away or stay safe from
the invisible poacher no guard catches before it's
too late? No sword, club, or gun stops or kills it.
Only soap and alcohol but despite them it rages on.
It's a challenge keeping distant from the invisible.

Staying safe is a challenge thrown at us at all times
to test the limitations of human senses and resources—
trying to elude what we cannot see, smell, hear,
touch, or even know but lurks in ambush to check
our guardedness after insane budgets on ammunitions.

150

On This Eid Day

(May 24, 2020)

There's no "other" in our midst, faithful or infidel,
and I send warm greetings to my Muslim relations.
We are on the same side against the coronavirus.
I cherish them reinvigorated after thirty days
of endurance to better bear the lightness of being.
Today we are more of one family than ever before.

This Eid day there's no gathering or visiting but we're
together after denying the body to uplift the soul.
Today is Sunday too. Every day is a day of worship.
The Eid holds despite all odds; nothing arrests time
and the human spirit. We all rise with the cheerful sun.
We are all one and on this Eid day no faithful or infidel.

151

Lessons

We learn
from the fool
who drinks before the hunt—
we have to be sober to down the leopard.

We learn
from the wise
who follows prohibitions to the letter—
we must do all it takes to be safe.

We learn
from the fool not to act before thinking
and from the wise to hesitate to be prepared.

The fool learns too late
and shows gashes of a narrow escape, if lucky.
The wise learns early not to step into a blaze
and totally avoids the pangs of the pandemic.

Covid-19 displays the fool and the wise
for common folks to stare at and think.
Survival drives humans to learn to live.

152

Waiting for Heroes (or Shylocks!)

(May 25, 2020)

The experts say only a vaccine can liberate us.
Everybody's waiting, praying to all the gods
amidst fear that rising tallies would climb over us.
There's a race in labs to liberate us from the virus—
some want to be richer than the richest they have been;
others won't mind being hailed as heroes of the poor.
Everybody waits in fear and the world won't care:
the steep price corporate ones will demand for immunity
or some fellows really putting science at the service of all.
Everybody waits for a vaccine to liberate us
and it's coming out of over eighty funded labs.

153

After Partial Lifting of the Lockdown

(May 26, 2020)

I left the house this morning
to gather resources for the day.

Day is a clearing I entered to seek my desires
after weeks of lockdown made me behave like
a prisoner of conscience liberated into a crisis.

I left the house this morning
to gather resources for the day.

I was freer at home in self-isolation
than masked and keeping distant from folks
in the tic-tac-toe of keeping safe in freedom—
a communal puppet to be six feet from others.

I left home this morning
to gather the resources of the day.

I brought nothing back after tedious hours
of perambulating to exercise freedom.
I knew in the ten weeks of self-isolation there
was so much I didn't need in my life for survival.

I left home this morning
to gather the resources of the day.

It was joy to step outside only to suspect others
but really needing so little to change my life.
I came back with trepidations of exposure.

I left home this morning
to gather resources for the day.

154

Join Me in Looking at Them

(May 27, 2020)

Another black man* can't breathe
police-choked and dies; protests follow
and life continues till yet another victim.

They lifted the lockdown,
unlocked the ferocity of bears
that bare their fangs in the street.

They have started shooting again,
they reopened crimes against humanity;
they uplifted the lockdown on hate.

Straights are taunting gays out of closets;
innocent ones convicted for crimes they didn't
commit and sentenced to life without parole.

They are expelling poison from their guts;
they lifted the lockdown precipitately
when humans have not shed their viral evils.

Don't hurry to incriminate the innocent,
don't hurry to rob the poor;
don't hurry to crush the conscience of the world

before totally lifting the lockdown,
before pouring hate into the street. Let there be
progress first on human treatment of other humans!

* George Floyd, a black man, died in white police hands in Minneapolis, Minne-
sota, and that led to protests there, across the United States, and the world against
racism and police brutality.

155

Ifs

If we all knew the novel coronavirus would flare up
to terminate the supreme-oiled performance of globalization,
individuals and the public would have avoided many regrets.

If I foresaw the viral flu and the lockdown ahead,
I would have completed fantastic deals in my favor
with hedges and bets as others then would be in a blindfold.

I would have left the decisions of separation to time as always
to resolve without rancor rather than be too smart for myself.
If I realized that decisions are good or bad depending on time,

I wouldn't have taken and signed loans that only a week later
would have freed me from the IMF cut-throat
but now depress me more than fear of the virus.

If two decades ago we knew there would be this,
the millennial hoopla would have been averted
and not wasted money to prevent a crossover crash.

If only a year ago the partisans of breaking away
knew we would be dejected and alone in the wood,
we would have chosen to remain in the union.

Many ifs, if we knew the coronavirus would strike;
if we foresaw the novel flu and the lockdown ahead
would bring the world to this state we had never been.

156

The Likes of the Coronavirus

(May 28, 2020)

The likes of the coronavirus will always spring from nowhere.
There's no time limit for hubris; a hundred years is nothing
to deflate the boast of eternal power, wealth, or ever-readiness.
The likes of the coronavirus will always be out there to discover
the Achilles' heels of exterminators after decades of probing—
a blind spot avails the coward chance to catch the leopard asleep,
deal it a death blow to carry home on the shoulders as a hero.
There will always be a time for the likes of the coronavirus
to call off the bluff of demi-gods hoping to be Gods on earth
and incapacitate them to the extent of making them laughingstocks
of generations of history only they once wrote and in their favor.
There will always be unarmed liberators to dethrone tyrants
who promulgate decrees of lifetime presidency of their misrule.
Interestingly, the likes of the coronavirus will cleanse the globe
to rearrange everybody and nation in a changed configuration.

157

Not Too Soon

Covid-19 is storming worldwide
into and from every direction at the same time
and that's the mystery of its power; the invisible poacher.

My 92-year-old mother broke her leg. Reduced to
an invalid, the sort Covid-19 loves to pluck down
in its forays. Age itself is an underlying condition

since my people acknowledge that old age is a disease.
The diseased tree will litter in a monumental storm
and afraid for my mom I tremble thousands of miles away.

A son owes his mother so many things.
I pray and wait for the tree not to fall too soon;
and not in the raging storm of Covid-19.

158

Some Police Are Crueler Than the Coronavirus

(May 29, 2020)

Some police are crueler than the coronavirus
and racism is the pandemic the superpower
should fight with all its resources to eliminate.
A white policeman with hands in his pocket
as if trained for gruesome murder all his life
knelt on a neck and despite "I can't breathe!"
said over and over again pressed life out of him.
This vile act makes coronavirus preferable
to the existential foe nurtured with bestiality
that sees black lives cheaper than a dog's or
cat's he seeks to validate a depraved manhood.
The coronavirus takes the old to their ancestors
but this police wipes out a black from growing.
And think of it, a white boy officer of the type
could halt and handcuff me outside for no reason
and perforate me as George, Breonna, Ahmaud, etc.
Despite the intolerable losses to the coronavirus,
the racism of many policemen is a worse pandemic.

159

Caught in the Act in a Period of the Coronavirus

(May 30, 2020)

Nine minutes in the act choking a human to death
by who's entrusted to be guardian of justice
caught with no effort to conceal brazen murder.
And follow days of raucous protests in the street
in the midst of the raging coronavirus pandemic;
the indelible blotch of racism America lives with.
If the worst affected in fatality numbers on earth
and now the habitual sins of history rear racist heads,
what can be said of power and wealth that the virus
has mocked with its fierce forays and diminished?
It's strength to slaughter the demons of raging racism
and not parade the unending litany of rabid killers
of innocent and unarmed but because of their color.
Nine minutes in the act of killing, days of fiery protests
show they're weak and poor the so-called powerful—
it cannot be strength to kill the innocent and unarmed;
it cannot be powerful to kill under cover of a uniform.
And so no efforts to conceal the brazen murder, and he's
caught in the act in a period of the raging coronavirus.

160

Truths & Lies Inc.

If you see the truths and the lies embedded in the coronavirus,
you'll also see why history can no longer be only written
by conquerors validating their conquests and empires of wealth
but now a chorus of tormented souls can be heard across borders.
With the invisible one dethroning mastodons of politics and purchase
and leaving thrones throes infested with programmed killing bees,
humans have carried more than the godheads of beasts and want
to relish their bestiality but cannot cast off what's their second nature.
The virus validates those against it with values but not morals;
hence the racists still rabid are killing in the streets in daylight
now without guns but suffocating victims and cameras catch them.
If you see the truths and the lies embedded in the coronavirus,
you worry why the ark cannot leave behind the beasts defiling
humanity with beastly acts and brazen murders under skin cover.
Truth and lies remain strategically embedded in the coronavirus
and we can see for ourselves the future of the world in its past.

161

Coronavirus Pales Before Racism

(May 31, 2020)

Today the coronavirus pales before
the rising statistics of blacks dead from
racist police killings ironically hiding
under law enforcement to escape justice.
The ethnic cleansing ones supersede
anything the virus has done in the land.

Today the virus is not only at the margin
but shoved to a blind spot amidst outrage.
Racism is a most cruel and lethal disease—
the raging coronavirus subsumed in fires
of race protests will further fuel things for
a toll of not only blacks but everybody too.

The coronavirus pales before the killer of centuries
that racism has done to slaves and buffalo men.
Folks no longer fear viral infection and march out
defiant of protocol, defiant of further police murders
to throw Molotov cocktails at racist property.
Today the coronavirus pales before systemic racism.

162

Positive or Negative for Racism

This contagion is so rampant
it's high time they tested each cop's
status for positive or negative in racism
before letting any of them out to their beat.
The casualties of racism are uncountable.
Every cop should be tested; those already
rabid should be sedated and sent to sleep.
Positives should have their contacts traced
and only through tough measures will killers
in police uniform be eliminated from the land
because the deadlier contagion is racism
with a million fatalities over centuries; not
the virus with over one hundred thousand.
It's high time they tested every cop
because racism is such a vicious contagion.

163

At the Confluence of History

While the coronavirus redirects history's path
to where nobody's sure of what will stand or fall,
another story, George Floyd's fatal choking, enters
and there are more fires in four days across the land
from protesters against racism than would burn from
American arsenals dropped in a premeditated war.

Two stories at the confluence of history—
one originating from China, duplicitous trade rival;
the other in Minneapolis, new epicenter of police murder,
the apoplexy of slavery and racism in a democracy.
At the confluence of these two stories, politics as
expected fuels both sides raising the toll of casualties
and guts the human conscience that should liberate all.
One murder challenges Covid-19 for the same place in history.

164

Why Should I Not?

(June 1, 2020)

Why should I not take risks with Covid-19;
why not join protests against police murder of Floyd
to register my conscience against the evil of racism
despite the raging novel coronavirus?

What causes more havoc to the land and people:
the coronavirus with its tally of over a hundred thousand
or because of systemic racism the many millions that
have died in all the centuries of a nation's independence?

What poses more danger to human existence:
the virus that can be managed and a vaccine can eliminate
or the total disregard for blacks and their lives
by those hiding behind their own skin to kill others?

Why should I not risk a season's pandemic
to wipe out racism, the endemic epidemic;
why should I not settle the perennial problem
before the season's bother over health and jobs?

If both the coronavirus and racism bring death,
why not allow me choose what to die for—
be a hero forever by stamping out racism, or
defying what has only 2% chance of killing me?

165

Images

There are some things whose graphics freeze in the mind—
New York bodies gurneyed into freezing trucks and dumped
into mass graves that continue to haunt with their grimness.
Now a Minneapolis police with his knees pinning a black man
by the neck to the ground despite his gasping "I can't breathe!"
with three accomplices watching and a pleading public nearby.

These images mark these moments indelible—the mass graves
and the infernos in American streets and worldwide protests;
the fear of who next to call for the ambulance and now I ask,
"Will I be the next black man killed by the police or who?"
both scenarios reminding me of the ancestral journey of no-return.

Protesters wield cameras in self-defense to record and bear witness.
The images recall human history; we no longer need armchair historians
or writers as these pictures freeze in our psyches for as long as we live.
Fortunately, we see for ourselves the unfolding history
in which we participate and bear individual and public witness.

166

Nobody Is Fooled

(June 2, 2020)

Nobody's fooled
that the flu from Wuhan is gone
or left its mischief spreading
because of the fires blazing in streets.

Nobody's fooled
that the mad mass response
to a systemic race murder pattern
there for centuries of a nation's history
also eliminates the novel virus
mapping its own movement and where
next to peak or start its second wave.

Nobody's fooled
that first things first. Racism, American cancer,
has to go; better burn down the nation to rebuild
to remove the centuries-old malignancy
than put time to the Wuhan flu for which a vaccine is in the offing.
Racism has no vaccine and devastates the conscience of a nation.

Nobody should ever be fooled
that the masses in the street against murderous racism
don't fear the flu, the new disease on the block;
but first things first: expunge the centuries-old cancer!

167

Truth is Colorless

There they stand: black, white, and brown
carrying posters against racism and murder.
They express the conscience of a proud nation
and in unison affirm what's true has no color
as what's a lie also has no specific color.
There are good and bad folks of every color
and the conscience of those fighting a virus
has no color as an armor against infection;
it only has to be clean, all around sanitized
irrespective of whether white, black, or brown
like those marching there carrying posters.

168

Rainbow Waves

(June 3, 2020)

It must be the three months of the pandemic
sensitizing all humans to the rude awakening
of everybody's mortality before the virus and
youths massing out with one song on their lips
that give me hope as never before in this land.
Those filling the streets with their presence raise
my hope that now there's neither we nor they;
the classification that for centuries divided folks.
For once every race is aggrieved by callous murder;
none can bear anymore unequal treatment of others;
hence youths of all races march in solidarity for justice.
I thrust my fist to stab the air to salute these marchers.
The rainbow waves of those against evil of every color
raise my hope for justice and that at long last we may
have arrived at the destination without us and them
but we all are offended by injustice and bonded together.
It must be the pandemic that has done this as never before;
made us embrace justice; a color-neutral virtue.
This awakening normalizes my hitherto arrhythmic heart.

169

My Hair in the Pandemic

(June 4, 2020)

Each time I look at the mirror
I know I am under the spell of Covid-19
and how much the body can bear for life's sake.

My hair has gone uncut for four months;
overgrown like a forest on a knoll and reminds
me of the Afro style I flaunted a long time ago.
Now hair spilling into nostrils, nose, and ears,
I am a caricature of what I used to look like.

I weigh the barber's shop and threats of infection
and no-one tells me not to continue growing my hair.
Life doesn't owe the body maintaining all its parts.

There are so many cosmetics I can do without and be fine.
I know so much I can do without and still be happy—
happy about my health for which I can't risk going out.

Is my hair a patch of wiregrass, weeds, or even a nest?
Each time I look at the mirror, Covid-19 stuns me
with lessons I wouldn't have known without this threat.

170

This May Be It

This may be it—
the confluence of aspirations; what prophets
foretold for ages in riddles and people waited for.

This may be it—
at long last the slippery eel of freedom caught tight;
the endgame no longer a politician's path to power.

This may be it—
the pandemic so chastened people's consciences
everybody experiences an epiphany to do the right thing.

This may be it—
the answer to the riddle that for centuries
wise ones couldn't crack for all their knowledge.

This may be it—
those the virus granted reprieve
doing the same for fellow human beings.

A season of awakening as never before
after the pandemic prepared all for a new kinship;
and this may just be it!

171

Government, Corporations, and People

(June 5, 2020)

The government wants people to spend
their earnings to stoke the market,
the companies look to their stocks cresting
in a good market at the peak of Everest;
the people don't know their shopping spree's
because conditioned to spend as the good life.
When the market is at the center of everything,
who cares about ways of profiting from others?
Who really cares if the state sends poor folks
to work with inducements despite the coronavirus
and for many to die from rushing to make money
for the desperate companies and the government
to boast in figures about a healthy economy amidst
high fatalities from the pandemic that thrives on
the avarice of politicians and the business class?

172

Under Your Influence

(June 6, 2020)

Whatever happens today comes under your influence:

a wedding that in years to come will be remembered
for taking place in a sparsely peopled hall—no dancing,
speeches restrained, and the celebrants marionettes;

the death of a ninety-seven-year-old mother of my friend
whose memory will not be of the last-breed character
but hurried burial without the clan's weeklong celebration;

the graduation of the highflying student, gem for the future,
who couldn't walk to limelight to shake hands of the Chancellor
and strut across the stage in a gown like a peacock he should be.

You're in the picture, invisible but the reason for absences
and presences and the lack of one thing or another
that would have been an everlasting shine in memory.

It's you the coronavirus that looms everywhere over everybody
that shrinks before your menace; you're more important than
the celebrant that stands at the corner of your mysterious shadow.

You arrange every experience now according to your own protective
protocol and show humans that they cannot live full lives
when you're in vogue and curtail all excesses they crave for.

Whatever happens today comes under your influence.

173

For Vera Uwaila Omozuwa

Were it not for the closure of schools to stop the spread
of the pandemic she wouldn't be home for this fatality;
were it not for the state's inability to provide homes light
Uwa* wouldn't be in church to read and be savagely assaulted.

But it's not the Wuhan flu that committed the chilling assault.
A humanimal stole into the church to rape and bludgeon her!
A curse on who's so disrespectful of his mother's and sister's kind!
Let every man who does not separate himself from the monster
be cursed—he should not have been born to perpetuate villainy.

Today I think of Uwa who would have been studying at school
and not a church desecrated by the cursed manhood of one
whose savagery slaughtered innocence and decency of hard work.
We all need to separate ourselves from the monsters of men;
we must bring justice to Uwa and others done unspeakable acts,
castrate and jail perpetrators to make everyone do the right thing.

It's not the pandemic at all that committed this effrontery against
a young woman; it's not the closure of her school to avert infection.
It is not the church that opened doors for a student to come and read.
The state shares complicity in not doing hard enough to stop violence
against women; the police share in it that they couldn't do their work.
But it's the animal of a man whose phallus should be forever cursed.

*Uwa: shortened form of Uwaila

174

What It All Means

(June 7, 2020)

What it all means,
these crowds defying the coronavirus
in waves rising through streets worldwide
rallying against racism and injustice
and growing despite calls by politicians
in Australia and Britain* and race-silent ones
to protest in other ways than mass marching,

one's conscience is worth saving than the body,
standing with justice is worth taking risks for;
ideas of human solidarity travel faster than the virus;
fear of death pales before the courage to say no
to the thunder and firepower sustaining unjust laws
and embracing change and flowing with it for the true
kinship of human kind is better than resisting it
by keeping silent in the face of brazen discrimination.

What it all means,
these waves of defiance of the virus and politicians
rising to a flood of legislations
and conversion of abettors and silent ones
to dismantle or burn down the centuries-old racks
of racism and injustice to keep groups down,
let it all end so that we all begin anew as humans.

*The Australian Prime Minister and the British Home Secretary asked the protest-
ers to go home and use other means to protest.

175

Democracy at Work

(June 8, 2020)

The political scientist touted tiers
of legislation in a democracy
until the novel coronavirus arrived.

The president made his broadcast,
the governor had his say over the state;
the chairman controlled the council,
and the mayor stood for the city.
They often contradicted one another
and the people for whom these tiers
were created and given authorities
suffered from the confused response
of politicians maintaining their turfs;
nothing if others challenged them.

Some interpret the constitution as
giving them rights that wrong others
and expose them to fatal consequences.
The virus rages through cities, councils,
states, and nations; it has no borders;
the people bear the brunt of the struggle
to implement democracy to the letter.

176

History As a Hobbyhorse

History has ridden a hobbyhorse
of colors for centuries
and so performs lies as true:
pink white, brown black, off
brown yellow, and even red.
Who invented the color codes
built the hobbyhorse with which
millions have been crushed.
In the time of the coronavirus,
who can be silent as masses
assault the lies and injustice
of history's hateful hobbyhorse?

177

Racism is Worse Than Covid-19

Racism is a centuries-old pandemic
with its epicenter in the United States.
Its carriers see themselves as superior
and keep silent in the face of injustice.
One wonders if they have a conscience,
or, if they have, theirs thrives on poison.
Racism is worse than Covid-19 that
kills a very low percentile and leaves;
it has been there since decoders of colors
uplifted themselves and demoted others.
Many brandish it to discriminate,
torment, and kill more than a pandemic
that one can learn to live with; but none
can't be human accepting the racist virus.

178

For Ignatius Iwegbue

(June 9, 2020)

I have to refresh the voice of long ago.
It's the coronavirus
that has brought this about
after almost sixty years of separation
this reunion in the season of the pandemic.
It's the phone calls to keep away moments
of fear, the leisure the self-isolation afforded
for deep reflection; the standstill of the world
that allowed us to catch up with each other
that at last did it.
There's a good narrative out of the lockdown—
reunions from an impossible distance.
Days at Obinomba* together as Mass servers
would have been lost without this communion
we share worlds apart.
And it's the coronavirus
that has brought this cheer about;
brotherhood that has withstood decades.
I refreshed the voice of long ago.

*Obinomba: here St. George's Grammar School, Obinomba, in Nigeria's Delta State which the poet and Ignatius Iwegbue attended as young boys.

179

On the Cusp of Dawn

(June 11, 2020)

On the cusp of dawn devoid of race hatred,
awakening after the cleansing of the coronavirus,
there's access to facts that can no longer be hidden
in the global glare of prying social media—
cameras capture from different angles a murder
the type that has been done by police for centuries.

On the cusp of what nobody expected, not even after
the virus had settled and we threw the future to the winds,
come flares of incandescence in rainbow waves never seen—
protesters crying "I can't breathe!" swarm cities; statues of
slavers toppling; the conscience of the world taking a knee,
and legislations at different levels against dehumanization.

Something we have never seen before has started at last;
in place of a post-pandemic life of things upside down,
it's not face covers or social distancing but normalizing
because there's never really been white, black, yellow or red
folks anywhere; a new normal in behavior as never predicted.
A chorus drowns the pandemic hysteria in the cusp of dawn.

180

Face Cover

(June 12, 2020)

When in a face cover I smile,
who knows it's a grin or not even a smile?
Coronavirus smothers my cheerfulness
as it sobers my temperament; as if saying
"Don't be too happy in these days of my reign!"
I understand when I hear someone full of zest
on Wednesday, sick on Thursday, and dead by Friday!"
Tomorrow has always been a riddle
but not this far beyond human comprehension.
What emotions do I express in a face cover
when moods alter so often, joyful, sad, and just nothing?

181

Second Wave

(June 13, 2020)

The first appearance so mysterious,
it took by surprise and broke the myth of those
who boasted of preparedness for any exigency.
It poached quite a number; overflowing obituary pages.
As soon as it started to abate after we understood it
or began to have a grip of it, as usual folks
returned to old ways, as if they didn't know that
things had changed and life couldn't be as before;
too free for an unending season demanding protocol.
The second wave swept those who couldn't hold
themselves back, foolish in freedom like who rejoiced
about a battle still raging but they felt already won.
A second wave sweeps away survivors of earlier assault
and because underestimated, made casualties to prove
that the presumptuous are liable to disaster; and they got it.

182

I Sing To Myself

(June 14, 2020)

A year without the sun splashing light from the horizon,
a long entombment that shouldn't be taken as without reprieve,
will pass someday if one holds stubbornly to hope—

those handicapping months lost hiding from a mortal assailant,
sheltering indoors despite calls luring outside for capture,
will pay as long as hope holds in sacrifice for survival.

Coronavirus flexes muscles recruiting its fifth columnists
from the ablest tricksters of every land, politicians, and usurers,
and dispenses death to those too eager to let a good bargain go by.

I would rather live in darkness imaginable for a year
than walk the sun to every picturesque landscape or plaza
where buyers mob and infect from shoving to pick their desires.

The trickster-in-chief and all the accomplices are out there
in theatres, salons, bazaars, malls, and playgrounds and their
attendants sit or stand for fun and go home marked by the trickster.

I am getting old in a ritual chair that needs me for its potency,
I am restive in a room without doors and windows to shut out intruders
but I am happy I sing to myself songs that others would want to hear.

183

I Hold My Breath

(June 15, 2020)

I hold my breath
amidst predictions of doom for my homeland.
In the midst of gains in protests
with acknowledgment that black lives matter
and colonial statues toppling in European cities,
I hold my breath.
I hold my breath
amidst predictions of doom again
as if Africa has not had a surfeit of it.
If the coronavirus so far has only smacked
Africa so lightly and not close to Italy or America,
why these predictions of being its last settlement
where doomsday will foist its fatality flag
over low-income ones barely hanging to life?
I hold my breath.
Can for once doubters be proved wrong
and Africa's sun triumph over obsidian clouds?
It's not a matter of dodging the bullet.
Can the strike be so degraded on impact
that Africa remains standing and shaking it off?
I am waiting to exhale.

184

We Are Back Again

(June 16, 2020)

We are back to the crowds again;
a kind of adolescent madness of adults
flouting the smallest of gatherings,
six feet apart, and wearing face covers.
We are mad again, lawless enforcers of freedom
to whom a three-century-old document counts more
than modern science recommends for everybody's safety.
We are back to lives of frontier settlers
who saw themselves as living a charmed life
when in fact they succumbed fast to mild infections.
We are back again adults teaching adolescents what we can't
practice—discipline's hard to acquire; hence this unraveling;
a second wave averted for not the recklessness of the brave.
Even before some could walk, feeling so exceptional
they went a step ahead, took to running and in the process
of not following protocol like others took retarding missteps.
See the unprecedented fatalities anywhere in the globe!
We are mad again; too ahead for our own good.

185

Preserving Lives and Inheritance

The Ooni in a face cover looks like a masquerade;
the kind that should entertain him at festivals.
Ukuakpolokpolor wore a mouth cover and uttered
no word in public and fitted his mask to the waist;
now his attendants carrying the swords wear face covers.
No senior chief whispers to the octogenarian Olubadan
what to say because of social distancing in the palace.
Aalafin's chanters have praises muffled by their covers
as the Shehu's algaita trumpeters wheeze through a scarf.
Abroad an old queen flees her gold-laden palace to shelter.
An Asian monarch flew away with consorts and guards
in plane loads to a cold mountain in Europe to be safe.
Many cultures too slow to change have taken a jolt—
the coronavirus has made it easy for custodians
of these institutions that history has revered by requiring
change to preserve their lives and their inheritance!

186

Peter's Death

(June 17, 2020)

We heard of Peter's death and the news more than chilled all of us.
Every death hurts but this sudden one is most unsettling—
a fifty-five-year-old son departed as his mother breathed her last;
a wife quarantined in a sealed-off ward when her darling left.
Peter's passing intrigues not only his nationals but outsiders too
in a manner death has not rattled with its craft of poaching power.
He was a veteran fighter who knew how to bring down any warrior—
political saboteurs, investigative journalists, fifth columnists, and more.
As chief warrior he would summon his armed forces to overrun foes.
He not only fought his way into the presidency at a young age
but too overcame every effort to bring him down by the ballot;
he cared not how many cadavers he drove tanks over to win.
Not satisfied with constitutional limits, he sought a third term;
the battle tougher than anticipated. He wore charms, summoned
witch doctors to give him herbal baths to be more invincible.
Never lost, he was confident of defeating the Supreme Court.
The battle stalled and he discovered some other ways of ruling;
still president stepping aside and anointing and installing someone
that even if the world campaigned against would still win and he did.
Unknown to him a tiny foe he denied its presence—it brought laughter
when announced there wasn't Covid-19 in the land; no testing done.
The virus slipped into the fortified palace to tame who disrespected it.
Before you knew it, the warrior was infected and died of cardiac arrest—
nobody wanted to acknowledge the virus defeated the veteran warrior.
What a fighter! He vanquished his people, vanquished rivals and foes
only to be downed by a virus that to him didn't exist. A pity, he died.
Every mother and wife should pray for better luck of warrior men!
We heard of Peter's passing and the news more than chilled all of us.
Every death hurts but this sudden one is most unsettling.

187

Other Lives

(June 18, 2020)

It takes living to appreciate life
not only of fellow humans
but also of non-humans.
There are always others
in our midst or out there
that we need to acknowledge
to be full beings. We contribute
to each other's existence.
See lives of my neighborhood
after the rain: trees drenched but fine;
birds dialoguing in strange tongues
as mine must seem to them too;
and all these others that make me
cherish my living at this time.
I see the beauty of leaves,
the unique texture of every bark,
and the soulfulness of these neighbors.
Not even human neighbors I don't know
compare. These don't know me too
as I don't know their stories in the open.
These neighbors give me a lift every morning
and make my day a triumphant parade
I look up to for others and me as one.
It takes living to appreciate other lives.

188

Those I Know

I know many who narrowly escaped.
I called to congratulate them in muted celebrations;
mauled, they missed by a sliver separating life and death.
I know others brushed by the ogre's shadow and scared
but felt there was no fatal consequence on their way.

Nobody I know so far has gone down the pandemic's maw.
Two friends departed at ninety-two and eighty-eight;
it was more of their time had come rather than it was
the virus that plucked them unripe in the wrong season—
Osonobrughwe,* bless them ancestors in a new world!

Nobody I know has been snatched by the viral hawk
at will as a chicken from the ground into the clouds.
Let us remain always invisible to the invisible poacher!
Let it pass by till a cure or vaccine arrives to fortify us
to not only blunt its carnivorous assault but also kill it!

*Osonobrughwe: Urhobo for the Supreme God.

189

Untouched

Many lives remain unruffled.
I have been fortunate this far
but these neighbors don't share
the record tremors and insomnia;
they are spared my human anguish.
I don't know their stories as they mine
of making amends to them like others
I offended but want to live with in peace.
Will sunbird, pine, or squirrel die
of Covid-19? We have separate trials.
Some resist by standing on the same spot
and others have to move about for life.
Many lives remain unruffled; others tremble.

190

Prayers Are for the Living

There's still a long stretch to the end;
weeks and months beyond the striking power
of the foe we cannot fight with jet fighters.
There are many trials and challenges
before a cure or vaccine arrives safely
to disrespect what has humiliated humans;
its name on every lip in the same language.
Osonobrughwe, take us through the pursuit
to where we can chant without concern:
Ewewu! Ewewu! Ewewu!*
Prayers are only said by the living.

*Ewewu!: exclamation of joy in Urhobo chanted thrice to designate a narrow escape
of serious danger as of death.

191

Waiting in a Time of Pandemic

(for J., June 19, 2020)

Love at this time seems to be at a stasis—
neither here nor there but really there and here;
all desires condensed into articles of faith.

Sunbird and bluebird out separately
nested in the sun and blue; love apart
but clinging to themselves from distances.

There's a song pouring from their beaks;
a longing in sight they sing as naked blues
and bask in suns that give them turns.

None is blind to the limits and the dream
of evaporating days and distance between them
to refresh songs now ditties of diurnal prayers.

When you are apart and clasp over a void,
tomorrow brings close the steps left ahead;
still a long wait before reunion's a reality.

It is always worth waiting in these times.
All the while love has abundant space
to nurture in the very depths of nostalgia

and what we wait for acquires a special flavor.
So, let's keep waiting as we must. The siege
will lift and then our hands will be as free birds.

192

In the Covid-19 College

(June 20, 2020)

I take back my boast—
not as strong as I bragged about;
since I can be floored by a power I didn't know.

I take back the toast of learned—
not as knowledgeable as I thought;
there's just so much about life I didn't know.

I take back my lamentation for denials—
I am far better off without wealth and property
to add tons of burdens to my pandemic worries.

For long too tight, I lower my guard—
my foe's not a hulk of a bully in the hood;
it isn't the witch I feared would poison me.

When I walked, I had been too slow;
I ran and I was too fast for myself—
destiny caught me at the right spot.

I now know where I belong in the order of things.
I am not in any way set apart from others.
I am only a leaf, not even a branch, and not the tree.

193

Frequent Flyer

For a frequent flyer whose flights
the coronavirus aborted abruptly,
I take walks in the wooded neighborhood
studying birds and their patterns of flight.
I also study clouds I can no longer break through
into a stratosphere to glide faster than sound.

My passports are of no use keeping me uninfected
and my transnational credentials futile; self-styled
Afropolitan stuck with Americans waging this
uncoordinated war against the novel coronavirus.

For a frequent flyer whose adventures
the virus aborted to spite my schedules,
I am standing on terra firma happy alive
and enjoying birds flying past singing,
watching clouds drifting changing colors.

I used to live in the air but here I am down.
Nowadays I am a child again flipping
through picture books of plane models.
At other times I play with my grandkid's
toy planes when they are glued to phones.

I am unable to take off, not to talk of flying.
I stare at the clouds unable to break into space
because the coronavirus aborted flights
and I lost my Platinum status and other
privileges I enjoyed in being airborne at will.

194

The Pain of Prophecy

(June 21, 2020)

Who foretold the coronavirus would come
to sow fire seeds of fear and fatalities
would have been executed as an alarmist
like Ominigbo* before the burning of Benin.
But here we are months into the ravages
of a virus that defies cures and upsets all.
None foretold the plague of an invisible one
because the world's so much scared of truth
that it shuts down any unsettling predictions.
But disaster will come abruptly anyway
despite looking away or shutting eyes from it.
They executed Ominigbo for sowing fire seeds
of fear to scare the Oba into flight from home.
That was just before a column of white ants
(a deep metaphor they salvaged) ravaged Benin;
and amidst flames took him away to die in exile.
Generations after, divined truth bristles in a dark
purview of tomorrow but no one dares say it out.
And many die when the powerful presiding over
republics that are kingdoms do not want to be scared
of a pandemic and truth and diviners the first to die.

*Ominigbo: the diviner who foretold the sacking of Benin (1897) which came true
after he was executed for scaring the Oba. Diviners of epha (evwa) in the Pan-Edo
region invoke Ominigbo before they cast their cowries or shells to affirm the cour-
age of telling an inconvenient truth.

195

Another Day

(June 22, 2020)

Another day has come.
Though there's fear too thick to think through
and impedes the breath from smooth flow,
still it's a reprieve that life wins every day.

I do the same morning walk and other rituals
holding back desires from tripping
and accelerating hope for tomorrow
in the war to overcome the coronavirus.

I know not when the raging infection will end
even though every day draws victory closer—
today takes steps to tomorrow in the prayer
to lift one wholly through fears of tipping over.

Day or date matters not in the pandemic calendar
with every breath troubled by uncertainties.
I celebrate today for breathing however ruffled.
Today's just another day of hopeful rituals.

196

Branches of Beauty

(June 23, 2020)

In my wooded neighborhood
the branches compel my attention—
they give every tree majesty and glow
bearing leaves, flowers, and fruits.
They are to trees what feathers are to birds.
A variety of branches stare at me;
each plant with its special formation.
I take in the cartography at work;
the spacing, symmetry, and equilibrium.
Here's nature's art unparalleled; chief
designer at the height of inspiration.
My vision improved beyond 20/20
with the pandemic and lockdown.
It's not that these branches weren't there
but I hadn't seen what I see now.
I see a world of only beauties, branches
that enthrall my walk with epiphanies.
Without these lovely branches around,
I would have missed this consoling respite
in the season of the novel coronavirus.

197

It's Nobody's Turn

(June 24, 2020)

It's nobody's turn to die
when the staggering number of fatalities
stuns the statistics of daily publications.
Yes, ICUs ration oxygen and ventilators;
yes, nature puts a limit to every lifespan,
but the coronavirus has come to unsettle
known protocols of life and death.

It's nobody's turn to die.
The coronavirus and death are sworn allies
in their poaching craft of invisible assaults—
they leave everybody unprepared the more they take away;
they also conscript destiny to their side
to make humans as helpless as they can be.

It's never been anybody's turn to die
before and now however the statistics go.

198

Breaking Bad News in a Time of the Coronavirus

(June 25, 2020)

"Is this a good time to talk to you?"
and you know there's bad news
because good tidings come in a rush and uninvited.
A deep breath and tension connects caller and called.
"Eehm." The hesitation's disquieting—
good news needs no delay to be delivered;
happiness a thunderclap you don't prepare for.
Boom! It falls. "I don't know whether
you have heard." That elicits no response
but a deeper breath. No progress made yet.
"Yes, I just have to tell you." No shout of
"Tell me now!" "Ok. It's rather bad news"
which the person called knows all along
and imagines the worst—a death of course.
The receiver narrows down the possible ones
so close who could have been struck this time,
thinking of the sick—the old, relative or friend;
he knows the grand poacher surprises so often.
"Tell me who!" he bursts out amidst the quibbles.
"Davidson!" Not familiar with that name,
he retorts "Wrong number!" and exhales;
spared another bad news but utterly shaken
again in the season of the coronavirus.

199

Season of Reckoning

(June 26, 2020)

It's the grim season of the pandemic
but it's not only the statistics of positive and negative
and the intolerable toll of the viral assault.

It's also the vociferous season of mass outcry against racism
that's the fabric of rich and powerful nations for centuries;
the falling of statues of slave owners and traders that breathed
freely in the open where innocent ones couldn't breathe;
the catching of callous police in their acts of serial murders.

This is more than the season of the pandemic.
It's a time of knowing where people stand—
the personal freedom crusaders with benumbed conscience
when it came to caring for what happens to vulnerable neighbors;
the fierce defenders of protests there and not here;
the double standards we have been living with for so long.

It's the grim season of the pandemic.
It's also a time to know where everybody stands,
and better still this is the season of reckoning.

200

Sting

(June 27, 2020)

Today the coronavirus stung close.
My son's test came back positive.
We await the nature of the infection;
for now he feels only a slight fever
but we know the poison is brewing
inside him like the flowering of evil.
We, for contact, go on quarantine
praying his youth will stall the super-
active invader and he will overcome it.
For now, we can only pray for him
to wear out the foe for us to celebrate.
Today the coronavirus stung close;
my son positive and we quarantined.

201

The Sins of the Children

(June 29, 2020)

The sins of the children can pass to their parents
in the season of the coronavirus pandemic and so
it's their responsibility to keep their parents safe.

My careful son gave a ride to his carefree sister
who flew in for a needless party; the origin of the sin.
They both tested positive and went into isolation;
everything quiet before an ambulance roared in
to pick them from another side of town and I heard.

Coronavirus makes parents pay dearly
for the sins of their children
and it's only a miracle they did not stay
long enough after their outing to infect us.
We must have had a narrow escape.

202

Imbalance

(June 30, 2020)

We wish the affairs of life are balanced.
If you burn clay, it hardens into terracotta.
If you moisten the soil, it is soft for growth.
If cautious, fish, game or man escapes capture.

But things aren't always balanced in life.
There're errors despite the best calculation.
There's so much poverty despite hard work.
There's infection despite all done for health.

We don't know the role the Almighty
and one's destiny play in this; lucky or not.
Things aren't always balanced in life
despite good wishes we want to come true.

203

When the Coronavirus Comes to the House

(July 1, 2020)

After son and daughter get infected,
the coronavirus really comes not just close
but home—it's no longer a question
of why allow in your children from outside
since reckless youths can wreck one's health.
It's an unexpected sting, if not a terrible stab
and you test with results coming in 3-5 days.

Every passing day lightens the torture
but no total relief till after twelve days.
It's like expecting an ambush anytime?

It's so close when house members out as adults
return for a day that has jeopardized four months
of stringent denial to keep the home impenetrable.
Now there's so much racking as never before—
the virus is real but the possibility of bringing
it into my home where I shelter a nightmare
it takes two full weeks to wake from and exhale.

204

Their Interpretation of Freedom

(July 2, 2020)

The interpretation of freedom frightens me.
Their Constitution granted them freedom;
hence they disinherited and enslaved others—
that was a license to turn virtues upside down.
They say their God gave them freedom and that
meant arming to shoot at will those of other races;
sitting on the downtrodden for centuries of freedom.
Their devil would do the same under the circumstances.
There's freedom to put into a rack those different.
Their freedom to misbehave frightens me
as they carry guns to protest against lockdown—
they don't ask themselves why they are so behind
the rest of the world; so free and rich and yet poor.
So, their interpretation of freedom frightens me
to take cover at home from those who cannot
wear face covers to save others, those who claim
freedom to go against the grain of responsibility
and care not if the rest of the world perishes
in the freedom they want to exercise blindly.
Their unregulated freedom frightens me.

205

The Limits of Freedom

(July 3, 2020)

It occurs to me
in the midst of the pandemic
harrowing body and mind

that those taking advantage of their skin
to espouse personal freedom they deny others
and cause mayhem to many—
the old, vulnerable, and helpless—

are so self-centered in exercising rights
that privilege them in the uneven society
they have worked to create on earth
they trample the human rights of others.

Which is a stronger right, a personal desire
to be a nuisance factor spreading infections
or the majority's human rights to live healthy?

206

Hypocrites By Another Name

Within two weeks
those leaders who tried to pour cold water
to stop unending protests against all forms of racism
that they would spread coronavirus
and so should instead of massing out
go home and look for other ways to protest

are the new global champions whose rhetoric
inflames marches for freedom in Hong Kong!
The same leaders promise protesters refuge
and citizenship to have their personal freedom.
One pumps up supremacist rallies with tweets.

Remember they suffocated the Occupy Movement.
Who stifle cries against racism, a pandemic
of historic proportion, and praise freedom to hurt
have a name in the language of which they are
spokesmen. Hypocrites fuel every pandemic.

207

Beatitudes

(July 4, 2020)

The debt I owe to life
I should pay to all I see or come across—
trees I love with grateful eyes,
birds and all musicians of the wood;
I must pay for the uplifting orchestra in the air.

If I have to pay for the love
I owe the divine for escaping what haunted me,
I'll give out all I have and remain rich
with life of one blessed with good fortune.

If everybody in the house positive or negative
has crossed the red line alive and cleared,
I owe all for these lives to others
and not whine about what others owe me in cash;
theirs is the least of debts to worry about at this time.

I owe love that I summon with all my life;
I owe my life to the fates of narrow escapes.
And to all living and divine I pay with love
and all the resources that life lavishes on me.

208

On the Twelfth Day of the Quarantine

Every morning of the self-quarantine,
suspended in the 3-5 days of limbo
we have to wait for the test result to be
negative or positive, a judgment day,
I check partner and daughter with whom
I share the triumvirate of isolation and
expectation. How are you? Any problem?
No complaint from anyone today as yesterday
and we look to tomorrow at the far limit
of the 2-14 days when the virus can pop up.
Today is the twelfth day of the quarantine
but nothing is ever taken for granted
when dealing with the adept trickster.
We are fine and hope so throughout.

209

Fireworks

(July 5, 2020)

Last night unrelenting fireworks
to celebrate Independence Day;
the pyrotechnics enthralled revelers
as it kept awake who shunned it
at a grim time for reflection.

It meant nothing to the coronavirus
that has raised its stakes with gamblers
gathered at the Washington Monument;
it did not shake it and only sharpened
the appetite to be more voracious.

They put on fireworks fit to entertain
an emperor and his volatile subjects,
but meant nothing to the problem at hand—
only defiance of the invisible poacher by
a chief presiding over grand gestures; all he had.

210

Rejecting Silence

In a period of high mortalities
nobody wants to be taken for dead
and so jumps to answer phone calls.
Nobody wants to taunt bad omens
as the coronavirus harvests a bumper.
Rumor flies faster than sound nowadays
and, before you know it, the trail global
with phones and social media so plentiful.

You respond to calls not to be taken for dead.
You call those you have not heard from
for long who are likely to be interested in you.
Sometimes you have to call a frequent caller
whose voice you miss and there's no response
only to see the name splashed among obituaries.

Silence is so macabre in a pandemic
that the rugged hermit comes out
or through phone or social media
to be counted among the living.
I am not surprised that everybody
jumps to answer phone calls. Nobody
needs a bad joke in a pandemic
and we shout from our hideouts.

211

On the 14th Day of the 14-Day Quarantine

(July 6, 2020)

Not the kind to be footloose because free,
not of the exhibitionist stock because Covid-19-free,
or take any open and wide road because it is there,
on this 14th day of the self-imposed quarantine,
moments to leaving the prison house,
and allowed by conscience and not law to move out
I look forward to freedom tomorrow
and to keeping others from the ordeal of waiting.
I'll come out cleansed in and out; humbled, knowing
what it means to be imperiled and escape narrowly.

212

For the Record

(in memory of Yasin Moyo)

It was not the coronavirus
that killed Yasin in his parents' verandah;
it was the overzealous police that killed him
enforcing the curfew to curb the spread of the virus.
The police perforated his neck and heart
and he was only thirteen years old
loved by parents, neighbors, and schoolmates.
As often happens in police murders,
a cover-up; statements without a bite
and nobody held accountable.
The police in uniform professional killers
murdered the thirteen-year-old who had less
than 0.25 percentage chance of dying from the virus.
It was the police in Yasin's neighborhood
that killed and brutalized folks and not the coronavirus.
And this testimony for the record to memorialize Yasin—
a thirteen-year-old schoolboy killed by police bullets
in the parents' verandah in Nairobi's neighborhood.

213

After the 14-Day Quarantine

(July 7, 2020)

With the two-week-sentence over, the door
opens outside to taste a life of adventure.
Freedom requires responsibility in return.
Also memory of quarantine after testing
on letting in errant children and neighbors
reminds one that narrowly escaped a trap
looking ahead and minding steps everywhere.
The first case is an error; the second folly.
The fear of catching infection rattles the mind
and I go underground to avoid playing
with the coronavirus raging and many falling.
I barter freedom at whatever price for safety.

214

Cynical Voices

(July 8, 2020)

More and more cynical voices call
for all to learn to live with Covid-19
if it continues to embed in our lives
like a spouse out of control but there.
Instead of fighting it to a fall, politicians
bend to pressure, open up businesses,
and further imperil the population.
Many throw up their hands in surrender
rather than fight on towards winning.
Living with the evil trickster as partner,
one might as well couple with the devil!
They who throw doors open more and
more espouse living with their foe
instead of wrestling it to a hard fall.
What life tangoing daily with Covid-19
instead of eliminating it from one's presence?
What happens to the warrior spirit we were
born with? Don't give up or yield to fear!

215

CV

(for Binta; July 9, 2020)

When my Francophone friend
in a chat box wrote about CV
dispersing fear all over Mali,
it took me time to realize whom
she meant; an obnoxious politician
as there are everywhere nowadays
whose names add to his notoriety.
After all CV wasn't my resume
but the trickster who's *Coloravisus,*
Koro, Corona, or whatever inflection
made it strange; a pseudonym
that's a euphemism for a mortal foe
hiding but all-seeing and poaching.
Not every name needs to be called
at times of pleasantries and happiness
not to sour the occasion's sweetness
and the coronavirus is one such; hence
we continued chatting and laughing
over the other's grammar and phonetics
without CV casting a pall over our lives.

216

Made in China

Everything nowadays is made in
and exported from China
to every corner of the globe
and that includes the coronavirus.
Only they have the maintenance culture
of their products, since they know
the source of the materials
and should anything break down,
they fix it to a manageable state.
As for others elsewhere
the product arrives with trouble,
causes damage, sometimes irreparable,
and you complain in your language
without communication. You're stuck
if you can't do away with it.
You can't ship back to China
their export of a broken-down brand!
Capitalism has to adapt to Socialist ideology,
or the other way around; confused perhaps.
Still everything's still made in
and exported from China,
including the global coronavirus.

217

Conversions

(July 13, 2020)

When we first met a year ago in Ouaga*,
my Dogon friend wore jewelry of crosses.
I didn't ask but she told me she was Christian.
She went back to Mali after the film festival.
Soon raged the conflict between herders and farmers.
Amidst that came coronavirus to disperse fear and pain.
Then political protests pitched imam against president.

My friend surprised me yesterday with a video call
and I saw her head covered as never done before.
"I thought you were a Christian?" I asked.
"I am now a Muslim," she replied, smiling.
I don't really care if she lives as an animist.
There are too many dangers to flee nowadays,
and the virus makes us calculate which way safety lies.

*Short for Ougadougou, capital of Burkina Fasso

218

Dizzying Heights

The news is nauseating again;
the statistics climbing an unknown peak.
The darkness in the nation's exacerbated
by cultural wars fueled by a sick warlord
lethal because he defies known symptoms.
The news has become nauseating again;
the graph zigzagging to a dizzying height.

219

Test Result

(July 14, 2020)

Thirteen days after the test
came a snail mail
which I opened without excitement—
"Your test result was NEGATIVE."
Under the circumstances, it couldn't be anything else.
What could have set off a bonfire
on the second to third day after the test
has become stale by the thirteenth.
The sleep lost the first seven days
when tortured by the Chinese demon
cannot be regained; what's lost gone
in line with the rule of the coronavirus—
there's nobody to query and make sense;
it's of no use if the result is positive
or negative thirteen days after.
Surprisingly came a snail mail
thirteen long days after the test
with "Your test result was NEGATIVE"
no longer making sense of the quarantine.

220

As Happens in Human Affairs

July 16, 2020)

As happens in human affairs
there's morality
when one takes consolation
in good behavior—
the careful one escapes danger
and one wishes the world followed
that order all the time.

That's when hubris makes sense—
the coronavirus gets one
who vociferously denied its existence
and even taunted it
as mild as the common cold
succumbs to it through infection.
Deserved tragedy.

But as happens in life
there's the gray area—amoral;
neither good nor bad really
but happens when the good
meets the bad at the end
and the bad escapes consequences
expected of it and triumphs.

We would like to have rewards
for good work and reprimands
for what's not done right
but as happens in human affairs
when we seek a clear-cut judgment
of right or wrong things get mixed up
irrespective of actions or omissions.

221

What Normal Return To?

(July 19, 2020)

I wonder why the frantic efforts to return to normal
when normalcy is outmoded and going against the grain
as if nothing has changed and today is still yesterday.
Why return to old habits which made us believe that arms
and wealth were all when in fact we were weak and poor?
Why not live the science foisted upon us to survive?

I won't allow trees and their branches that gained so much
magnificence and enthralled me to lose the companionship.
Nor birds that mark my airspace with magic formations
and the orchestra of non-humans leave me without blessings.
What of the kinship of other races and beings I want to keep?
What normal return to that will give me this throbbing new life?

Let what I have gained this pandemic season not go away
but make me and others more human than in *normal* times.

222

It's No Coincidence

(August 5, 2020)

It's no coincidence that today rewrites the history in our books;
no accident that Floyd's murder enraged the world when it did.
It's not by chance that black lives now matter not only in America
but also in Britain, Australia, and elsewhere North or South. No fluke
that the police caught by camera and onlookers in acts of murder.
Not by chance that statues of racists and empire builders are toppling.

The confluence of rivers we see isn't the cartographer's making.
If it is ordained that despite all earlier struggles with guns failing,
current peaceful protests against armed hypocrites are succeeding,
it cannot be mere chance or accident. A time comes for success.
It's the season of the coronavirus and history's getting re-written
not by those who conquered others but a new force of conscience
that sees the atrocities earlier committed pale before this pandemic.

223

Pandemic Months

(August 25, 2020)

Should these six and more months
be riled as wasted
when indulgence should give life
an epicurean treat
or a brief era of waiting
denying oneself of quite a lot
testing loyalty to be stronger
and sharpening appetite
into a flame for reunion?

The pandemic months can be read
either way of waste or waiting
in a time like no other has been
but which we have no control over.
What's wasted that doesn't enrich
the sensibilities that drive the body
to gain more power for the future?
And what not wait for
these six and more months of hope
if that purifies and saves into a new being?

224

When Will the Pandemic Year End?

(September 12, 2020)

It doesn't seem as if this year
will end on December 31 when it should.
After all, the year of the pandemic didn't
start till WHO proclaimed it on March 11.
It's true it began earlier, perhaps February
when already known for what it would be—
a deadly draft in the annals of normalcy.
Oracles prophesy that the year of the poacher
would inevitably extend its grip till later—
a passing long snake with a head on either side.
The year of the pandemic has no clear start
and is shunning a specific ending. It came
from nowhere though Wuhan is somewhere
and it's acting deadly according to character;
exacting more than a monstrous mouthful
ignoring the December margin before ending.

225

War Fatigue

(September 15, 2020)

When war seems coming to an end,
things look so uneventful that
everybody suffers from battle fatigue
and one thinks things will fizzle out.

Then is when fire breaks out
and an implosion takes place;
sky aflame streets infuriated
and evacuations the only way out.

There are protests in town
complicating the streetscape
of shootings and arson—one war
turns into several unending battles.

When folks are tired of lockdown
and break protocol to be free
the flattened graph rises in casualties
and that's when there should be more care.

226

For Once

(September 17, 2020)

For once the experts seem wrong
despite the logic of their informed forecast.

The big belly of the mother continent
refused to turn into a vast graveyard.
The arch poacher of the new century
has found it hard to practice its craft
among those shielded by malarial attacks.

It has not happened: the total silence
of communities except for wails.
The aged in dirges still ride away in state
to join the ancestors in a festive mood.
Every tree holds tenaciously to unripe fruits
until the season of ripeness and falling.

For long bashed by centuries of foreign raids,
this time they stand their hard ground
and won't fall to what others wish them.
They counter the coronavirus with their spirit
and not reserves of pre-paid vaccines;
the unarmed survive the throes of the strong.

For once the experts are wrong
despite the logic of their learned forecast.

227

The Future of the Two Streets

(September 19, 2020)

Even when the vaccine comes
to raise stocks to the dream height of investors

the two streets of America won't be at peace with each other—
one healthy and happy; the other sick and morose

as fires, fumes, police and gang shootings won't
stop cadavers from skyrocketing and demoralizing.

228

Travels During a Pandemic

(September 20, 2020)

I travel by way of dreams
to untold landscapes
to meet novel beings that hadn't come my way.
That's what social media does—
brings to me the strangeness
of far places and what's been hiding beside me.
The lockdown didn't paralyze my legs
but offered me wings to cover more worlds
and another eye to penetrate thick clouds.
I learned so much of distant places
from my restriction to stay put here.
I travel to undreamed-of places.

229

Laughing at the King of Fools

(October 3, 2020)

Normally one would not laugh at another falling sick
but when normalcy is thrown to bulldogs to maul
what does one do
when what doesn't exist brings down
the commander of the mightiest army in the world;
what happens when the clown falls victim of his jokes?

Normally one should not laugh at the sick
but what does one do
when the arsonist is hospitalized for burns from the flames
he started and walked through to prove his invincibility?
What happens when the poacher is gored by the beast
whose population he endangered for personal wealth?
What happens when who prayed for rain to ruin others
cries for rescue from the mudslide burying him alive?

We should not laugh at the sick because it is human to fall sick
but what should one do
if one taunting the collective godhead of all humans
with the power of the constitution gets struck
by what the Greeks let out centuries ago—hubris?
One should not laugh at others sick
but who can resist laughing at the king of fools?

230

Like No Other

(October 7, 2020)

This year misses its rhythm
but it's still counted as one
that passes but like no other—
an aberration in the annals of
tradition as we know it.
The cock crows with a stutter;
the sun rises over pale faces
and the diurnal rust smacks life
with cold, lead, and dust.
This year misses the flow
of a hundred years
but of course it's still counted
like no other but 2020.

231

Folkloric Relatives in the Pandemic

(October 12, 2020)

I wonder how these figures, relatives of sorts,
would have fared in the coronavirus pandemic.

The tortoise cautious and cunning to a fault would stay
locked down in his shell for however long to survive.

The spider trying to keep all wisdom would lose so much
with too little left to hold him back from falling into deep trouble.

Eshu wouldn't mind sending mixed messages that would make
many to suffer or die while he stayed safe at the sideline.

Iphri so predictable would either roast the virus if it came close
or, rash and eager, blind himself from the invisible terror's path.

But we are all of these—tortoise, spider, Eshu, and Iphri
carrying careful and carefree features in the family genes

and would have been fortunate not to be directly targeted
by the arch poacher of human lives and escaped fatalities.

232

When Love is a Palliative

(October 24)

Don't behave as if there's nothing for me
as I waste helpless before your eyes.
You have in your heart something that nobody
suspects holds anything that can revive a man.

Coronavirus unleashed a war against all and with
every fiber each fights for life; drained or dying.
There are palliatives to survive the pangs
of this pandemic like no other we have seen.

My love for you is a war fierce like no other.
You hide the key to where there's refuge.
I will break in and seize for myself your love,
since you behave as if there's nothing there.

Brimming warehouses and folks still dying of hunger!
You say my happiness is your prayer and task.
I don't know if you really know what hurts me so.
I'll have it from you even if through looting.

233

From the Ventilator to Breathing on Her Own

"Amreghe's on a ventilator at the ICU"
shook me at 2:15 am like a thunderbolt.
The doctor had to let me know. "It's critical."
Far away and in days of no visits to relatives,
what do than summon Gods remembered in need?

The news dripped from updates of little change.
"They can't tell what's really wrong but she's positive."
This is coronavirus again after the previous scare?
Lightning strikes twice within a mere three months
and that situation of assumed immunity a hoax
makes everything mysterious and so perilous.

Silence is neither good nor bad; a mask of life or death.
"Her memory's affected and can't recognize people."
The sleep wasn't that deep though induced but she woke
to breathe on her own to be treated with anti-viral
and fever-lowering medications; a staple cocktail of the time.

The consecutive nights she calls at about 2:15 am—there's
daily improvement though slight; she's out of the ICU to another room.
This night I take a video call. "Daddy, where is Eloho?" "She's sleeping."
"Do you want to talk to Mommy" as I notice her stir in bed.
Though slow, she gets to talk to each of us as a family.
That's the relieving news of today.

234

She is Alone

(October 26, 2020)

She is there alone
wondering how she came there.
Calling at 2:15 am and amazed
the family goes to bed so early
because she can't tell what time
it is that late to be awake.

She can't remember familiarly
all the events shared.
Questioned to respond, she's silent
and when given the answer
mutters "Oh!" startled at the much
she has lost. She doesn't understand.

She is there alone
but with God, doctors, and nurses;
no visitor allowed in.
Later moved from the ICU to a step-
down room; a cause for relief but still
not aware of what she's going through.

When she calls on her own,
she remembers who of us three
has not talked to her.
She is getting out of the dark
alone in a bed she can't fathom
how she got there in the first place.

She is coming down the cliff
step by step but steadily
as we nudge her with remembrances
and we look forward to days ahead
of vibrant family chatter, after lonesome
days with God, doctors, and nurses.

235

Good News

(October 28, 2020)

Lightning struck fear into everybody.
It missed by just a sliver
to hit a tree under which she sheltered.
The news of a narrow escape gladdens.

Lightning hit the tree under which
she sheltered from a treacherous storm.
A hunch spirited her from the ominous pathway.
This song celebrates the narrowest of escapes.

236

Denied Entry

(October 30, 2020)

Denied entry into another world
she turns back
to first take a rest at a unit outside the ICU
with precise rites of daily regimens
for ten more days.
Each dawn brings her closer home
without further veering to the unknown.

She is closer back to us
Telephoning and watching television
after a respirator stopped her
at the point of no return.
She recovers her memory daily
and sharper as she undergoes the rites
her life relies on to be safe.

Alone she fell too far away
without a symptom
to almost cross the ethereal border
but promptly pulled back by gloved hands
and here she is in the familiar world.
Quite a narrow escape
for which we celebrate.

237

From the Limits

(October 31, 2020)

Better for others to underestimate you
than know the rock and fire at your disposal.

You unsettled Covid-19 and its death-dealers
and the monster force backed off.

They thought they could capture you
and take you away but you repulsed them.

They felt they could push you through an open gate
but you stood your ground and turned back from the limits.

Their ill wind came with a rush to snatch you away
but the deep-rooted wire-grass you are resisted it.

They saw you diminutive and underestimated your resolve
to survive but you astonished them with your loud "No!"

Far better they underestimate you and ill prepare for combat
than you mock them and make them over-arm to take you on!

238

Seduction

The nakedness of even trees
brings its own seduction to me
with their serene tone and candor
of bare limbs. They are clean to the pore.
Winter strips them clean to test my constancy.
I know spring will dress them up for outing;
green-coiffured and graceful
for me to yearn for other desires.

Their contours amazing from roots through trunk
to branches upon branches to stems,
they reach out to the sky
for the drafts that air and light offer.
Of course, we now know their true height
from their outdoor-groomed outstretched fingers
that attest to the tallness of standing figures
in a lithe physique; an upright kind.

What they now lose in glamour,
they make up for in trademark barks.
And they will tantalize with flowers,
fanciful fabrics imported from other climes,
when summer comes to smother with long sunlight
and they will blush in the fall wearing cool colors.
And these are the same neighbors I pass daily!
Their beauty possesses me every season.

Credit: Courtesy of the author

Tanure Ojaide was educated at the University of Ibadan and Syracuse University. He has published collections of poetry, as well as novels, short stories, memoirs, and scholarly work. His awards include the Commonwealth Poetry Prize for the Africa Region, the All-Africa Okigbo Prize for Poetry, and the BBC Arts and Africa Poetry Award. In 2016 he won both the African Literature Association's Fonlon-Nichols Award for Excellence in Writing and the Nigerian National Order of Merit Award for the Humanities. In 2018 he was a co-winner of the Wole Soyinka Prize for Literature in Africa. Ojaide is currently the Frank Porter Graham Professor of Africana Studies at The University of North Carolina at Charlotte.

ABOUT THE PUBLISHER

Spears Books is an independent publisher dedicated to providing innovative publication strategies with emphasis on African/Africana stories and perspectives. As a platform for alternative voices, we prioritize the accessibility and affordability of our titles in order to ensure that relevant and often marginal voices are represented at the global marketplace of ideas. Our titles – poetry, fiction, narrative nonfiction, memoirs, reference, travel writing, African languages, and young people's literature – aim to bring African worldviews closer to diverse readers. Our titles are distributed in paperback and electronic formats globally by African Books Collective.

Connect with Us: Go to www.spearsmedia.com to learn about exclusive previews and read excerpts of new books, find detailed information on our titles, authors, subject area books, and special discounts.

Subscribe to our Free Newsletter: Be amongst the first to hear about our newest publications, special discount offers, news about bestsellers, author interviews, coupons and more! Subscribe to our newsletter by visiting www.spearsmedia.com

Quantity Discounts: Spears Books are available at quantity discounts for orders of ten or more copies. Contact Spears Books at orders@spearsmedia.com.

Host a Reading Group: Learn more about how to host a reading group on our website at www.spearsmedia.com

Printed in the United States
by Baker & Taylor Publisher Services